THE
Simple
DINNER
EDIT

To the incredible Simple Home Edit community. You are my friends away from home and the reason I love what I do. This book is for you.

THE *Simple* DINNER EDIT

Nicole Maguire
of Simple Home Edit

plum. Pan Macmillan Australia

CONTENTS

Introduction

I love sitting down to a delicious, comforting meal at the end of a long day, but don't love the idea of spending hours in the kitchen making it. My favourite meals are those that are fast, achievable, made with simple and inexpensive ingredients, and which require very minimal prep ... if they're great for smothering with chilli oil, and I can eat them in my pyjamas and slippers, they get extra points.

I've always loved food and used to be an expert at dreaming up amazing family meals in the middle of the supermarket aisle. I would impulsively add ingredients to my shopping cart only to get home and find myself throwing out wilted vegetables at the back of the fridge that I'd fully intended using, but just didn't get to. I'd unpack the fourth bag of plain flour next to the two already open bags in my pantry, then end up ordering takeaway more often than I would like because meal planning for my family, plus cooking and washing up, was a mission. I was tired, I was spending a fortune and constantly wondering what to make for dinner.

Needless to say, it wasn't working! There had to be a better way ...

I worked hard to come up with new systems in my kitchen that save me money and time and also my sanity. I found that it's absolutely possible to eat delicious meals, just like those from many of your favourite cafes and restaurants, but you can do it all in the comfort of your own home, for a fraction of the price, all better quality and fresher, while spending as little time in the kitchen as possible ... because no one wants to be slogging it out in the kitchen every day of the week.

This book is filled with meals that your whole family will love to eat and, more importantly, that you will love to make. I've filled it with tips to help make your life easier, including recipes for meals that you can cook once and feed your family with twice, along with recipes suitable for batch-cooking and freezing (ready for when you need them). There are also ideas for meal prepping and food storage, to help you get dinner on the table quickly and effortlessly on those busy nights where time isn't your friend but you still want to be sitting down to something delicious at the end of your day. Plus, all the recipes include tips on what to do with leftovers.

I passionately wanted this to be a cookbook that you can use every day of the week, filled with a variety of mouth-watering, fuss-free, easy recipes, made with familiar, family-friendly flavours and accessible ingredients. Amazing homemade food doesn't need to be complicated (or expensive!) and the recipes in this book will help to answer that inevitable daily question – 'What's for dinner?' – all while doing it in a way that is affordable, helping you spend less time in the kitchen and giving you more time to enjoy with your family. You'll find comforting pub classics like Baked Chicken Parmigiana (page 74) and one-pan wonders like the 'Hidden Veg' Meatballs in Rich Tomato Sauce (page 67), as well as super-speedy dishes that you can whip up in 20 minutes flat, like the luscious Chicken with Creamy Mushroom Sauce (page 29) ... yes, all in 20 minutes!

The basics.

It's time to take charge of your kitchen

Meal planning

Have you ever landed in the supermarket, hungry and planning what to have for dinner on the fly, before getting to the checkout and realising you have spent a fortune? I sure have. Meal planning is a key change I made that instantly saw me saving money and removing the stress that came from the daily pressure of wondering what to cook. Suddenly there was no more waste. The impulse purchases stopped and I found myself eating the foods that I wanted my family and me to be eating, which everyone also loved.

Meal planning does not need to be complicated; in fact, the simpler it is, the more achievable and realistic it will be to maintain. Meal planning does not mean assigning meals to specific days (unless you want to). It's about being prepared, knowing what you will be eating that week and shopping specifically for those meals.

Meal planning tips

Inventory check

Shop your fridge, freezer and pantry before you go to the supermarket. This avoids unnecessary purchases and duplicate buys (because no one needs more than one paprika spice shaker open at a time – even me who uses paprika in every second recipe). What are the ingredients that you already have that you could use this week? Beef mince in the freezer? Loads of pasta in the pantry? A couple of carrots in the fridge? Maybe you could try a delicious Creamy Bolognese Pasta Bake (page 90) or easy 'Hidden Veg' Meatballs in Rich Tomato Sauce (page 67) to use these ingredients up. Are there a few sad-looking vegetables that need to be used fast? Maybe a 'catch-all' Quick & Easy San Choy Bow (page 158) is the answer. Is there a night where it may be beneficial to use one of the freezer meals you have made ahead of time? (See 'Get-ahead Sundays' on page 14 for more details.) You may surprise yourself with how much you can make with what you already have on hand. Make it a priority to use what you have first, to avoid waste and to save money.

Check your schedule

Check your weekly schedule and the family calendar before you meal plan. What is happening with work, what activities do the kids have, are there sports, are there days where you know you are going to be more tired than others or simply pushed for time? These are the days where you can lean into quick meals, the slow cooker, or prepped freezer meals (more on this in the following pages) to support you in these busy moments.

Core meals

Who wants to be thinking of new meal ideas every night of the week? Not me! The key to eating well on a budget is to keep it simple. Simple planning. Simple ingredients. Simple meals. Get input from your family and come up with a list of 'core meals' – the meals you know everyone loves to eat – and write them down. These are the tried and tested, go-to meals with familiar ingredients that you can rotate on your meal plan without much thought. When meal planning, give yourself a break and add these dishes to your meal plan first before choosing new recipes you would like to try out. As you try new recipes, your 'core meals' list will grow.

Once you have identified what meals you are cooking for the week, write them down. A menu board on the fridge is a great way to get the family involved and help with dinner, otherwise add your meal plan anywhere it makes sense for you (in your planner, calendar or simply as a note in your phone).

Save money on your grocery shopping

Save money on your grocery shopping by avoiding multiple trips to the supermarket (choose one consistent day per week) and shop seasonally. Plan your meals around produce and ingredients that are in season as they will likely be cheaper. Use supermarket weekly specials catalogues and create your meal plan around what is on offer.

Staples

Staple ingredients are those that you reach for again and again. For me it's items like flour, salt, cooking oil, apple cider vinegar, tamari, rice, crushed canned tomatoes, pasta, tuna, chickpeas, whole-egg mayonnaise, and the list goes on. There is nothing worse than cooking up a few sausages on the barbecue only to realise you have run out of barbecue sauce (or ketchup if that floats your boat). Or realising there is no baking paper for the zucchini slice you're about to bake. Having a dedicated spot to write down staples as they are running low will help you streamline your weekly grocery shop. I have a whiteboard in the pantry where I write things down as they run out, but a notepad or even a note in your phone is equally sufficient. These staples will be your first point of call when creating your weekly shopping list.

Shopping list

You've taken inventory, you know what staples you are running low on, so now all that is left to do is to write a shopping list with the ingredients you need to make the meals you have selected for the week.

Choose a start day

I know this may sound like 'a lot' and you are probably wondering when all of this planning and shopping is meant to happen. I'm going to share my routine with you, bearing in mind that there are no right or wrong options here. I have a young family with school-aged children, so for us it's important we are not starting Monday morning with an empty fridge. The day you choose to write your meal plan, write your shopping list and do your grocery shopping will all depend on your schedule.

Our family's meal plan runs from Saturday to Friday. I plan only one week at a time as it allows me to factor in any events and activities that come up. For us it's also important we have a full fridge of food over the weekend as not only does it mean I have time over the weekend to get ahead and prepare the food I've purchased (see 'Get-ahead Sundays' over the page), but it also stops the temptation of takeaway.

Wednesday Is the day that I take inventory of my fridge, freezer and pantry and finalise my meal plan and shopping list. I generally place an online grocery order to be delivered on Friday morning. This may not suit everyone, but I find online grocery shopping a great way to save money. It allows me to keep track of my overall spend as I add ingredients to my shopping cart, and it stops impulse purchases. I adjust meals on my meal plan accordingly if my total spend is creeping over my weekly budgeted amount. If my shopping cart is more than what I would like it to be, I ain't adding salmon to it that week, I'll add something more economical like beef mince.

Friday I have my groceries delivered or I head to the supermarket. I pack my produce away and my family helps with this too. I find it too overwhelming prepping my groceries on the same day so I usually reserve that for the weekend.

Saturday/Sunday I spend some time preparing my groceries ready for the week ahead (see 'Get-ahead Sundays' over the page for details).

Get-ahead Sundays

Weeknights can be hectic as we juggle kids, study, work, school, sport, housework, activities and all the other 'stuff' on our never-ending to-do list. I love dedicating some time in the kitchen on the days where I have an extra hour or two up my sleeve to reset and prepare for the week ahead. I pop a load of washing on and turn on some tunes before getting stuck into a few simple steps that give me back hours during the week and help mealtime run more smoothly, without consuming my entire weekend.

Food prep

There is no better way to control wastage than by spending a little bit of time prepping your food ready for the week … and I don't mean having every single vegetable cut and stored in individual containers ready for each meal – unless you want to. The food prep that I'm referring to is the basic prep that will ensure that the produce you are buying is actually being used and being eaten.

Recommended

Prepare the fruits and vegetables you are unlikely to reach for unless they are already washed, cut and ready to be used. Heads of lettuce, kale, cabbage, watermelon, pineapple, rockmelon, whole broccoli and cauliflower are all great fruits and vegetables that you can cut and store in containers, encouraging you to use them when you need them.

Nice to do

Cut snacking vegetables ready for use (see Food Storage opposite) and wash whole fruit ready for eating.

Elite

Batch-wash your fruit and vegetables so that they are ready to go come mealtime.

Fruit and veg washing tips

Berries Soak them in 80 ml (⅓ cup) white vinegar and 250 ml (1 cup) water to clean them and help them last longer. Rinse in cold tap water and dry thoroughly before storing.

All other produce Fruit and veg are best washed under cool running water but can also be soaked for up to 10 minutes with bicarbonate of soda. Bicarbonate of soda is an inexpensive, mildly abrasive, natural cleaning agent that helps to loosen debris and remove dirt and bacteria. Use 1 teaspoon bicarbonate of soda per 500 ml (2 cups) water and rinse your fruit and veg thoroughly in cool running water after soaking. Ensure fruit and veg are thoroughly dried (using paper towel or clean tea towels) prior to storing.

Food storage

So much time, effort and money goes into our grocery shopping and there is nothing more heartbreaking than reaching for the coriander you need for your delicious Thai beef salad only to realise it is limp and browned ... and you only purchased it two days ago. These are some simple food storage tips that work. You don't need fancy equipment or containers. These tips will help extend the life of your produce for multiple days.

Herbs

Wrap washed herbs in several damp paper towels or a clean damp tea towel before storing in an airtight container or reusable sandwich bag. This will extend their shelf life by multiple days (a minimum of 3 days). *Works with all herbs except for basil and mint, which brown when stored in the fridge – store these herbs in a jar of water (in a bouquet) on your countertop instead.*

Leafy greens

Washed leafy greens, such as spring onions, Asian greens (bok choy, pak choy, choy sum and Chinese broccoli), all benefit from being stored in a clean damp tea towel. Wrap the vegetables individually before storing them in your crisper. This method will extend their shelf life by multiple days (a minimum of 3 days).

Lettuce leaves

Wash lettuce leaves and use a salad spinner to dry them thoroughly. Store in an airtight container or reusable sandwich bag with dry paper towel on top and bottom to keep them fresher for longer (a minimum of 4 days).

Shredded cabbage

Thoroughly dry your cabbage leaves prior to shredding. Store in an airtight container or reusable sandwich bag with dry paper towel on top and bottom to keep them fresher for longer (a minimum of 4 days).

Snacking vegetables

Store snacking vegetables, such as cut cucumbers, cherry tomatoes, carrot sticks and celery stalks, separately in containers. Use a single sheet of paper towel on top of the vegetables (before covering with the lid) to absorb moisture and keep them fresher for longer (a minimum of 3 days).

Batch cooking

There is nothing more satisfying than coming home to dinner already made thanks to batch cooking, which allows you to make food ahead of time to enjoy later. You can batch cook by doubling the ingredients when you are making dinner. OR if you find energy levels are low come dinnertime, you may choose to allocate some time during the week where you cook a meal or two to help you get ahead. It's helpful taking your time, turning on some tunes, preparing your ingredients first and washing up as you go.

Choose the right meals

You'll find a whole bunch of freezer-friendly recipes in this book, many of which can be cooked once and eaten twice, repurposed into completely different meals. Curries, slow-cooker meals, pasta sauces, soups and stews all lend themselves to freezing.

Portion

Using containers that are the same size helps with portion control and ease of storage in the fridge and freezer. Liquid chalk is perfect for adding labels and dates so you can keep track of what you have.

Freezing and reheating

Cool your food before freezing and freeze within 2 hours of cooking. Most meals can be stored in the freezer for up to 3 months but I've included specific instructions for all the freezer-friendly recipes in this book, so you can enjoy your meals at their best. For them to remain at their best, meals should be thawed completely in the fridge overnight prior to being reheated.

Clear the clutter, clear your mind

There is nothing worse than moving mountains of paperwork off the kitchen bench before being able to get a start on dinner. Or having to dig around your utensil drawer trying to find the one wooden spoon that you use every day. Or having to hunt for the butter again because it hasn't been returned to the same spot. Or opening up a bag of rice only to realise there is already one open. Or trying to find the sponge to wash up, but having to wrangle plastic bags and other cleaning supplies under your kitchen sink that keep spilling out.

Clearing the clutter and organising your kitchen is completely free and is the key to cooking efficiently. Working in an organised space makes everything faster and effortless, from creating a shopping list and packing away groceries, to cooking and washing up afterwards. Having what you need on hand in a clutter-free environment ensures you aren't running around the kitchen hunting for your equipment or ingredients. Decluttering your kitchen may sound overwhelming but taking it one space at a time is the answer. A clear kitchen results in a clear, fresh mind, ready to tackle mealtimes.

Kitchen bench

I know from first-hand experience that the kitchen bench can quickly lure clutter and become filled with mail, keys, sunglasses, coins, rubber bands (where do they even come from?) pens and receipts.

Try a basket in your shoe cupboard for keys and coins, a tray in the pantry for incoming mail, or a catch-all drawer in your hallway console that gets cleared every few weeks. Finding a home for these belongings will bring about a sense of calm in your kitchen, which will in turn motivate you to use it.

Under the sink

If the thought of washing up after mealtimes makes you cringe, it may be worth assessing the area underneath your kitchen sink, which is often overlooked. It should be home to all of the cleaning supplies you use on a daily basis to wash your dishes and clean the kitchen. Your favourite supplies should be easily accessible and, if you're finding yourself opening those under sink cupboards only to find an excess of items spilling out, it may be time to remove some of the clutter. Remove double-ups or any cleaning supplies used for other areas of the home to another space if possible (like the laundry), and only keep the cleaning items that you use daily. It will free up space, make it much easier for you to find what you are looking for and remove some of the pressure from clean-up time.

Fridge

An overfilled fridge is the quickest way to land yourself in 'waste territory'. It's an area in the kitchen that can get out of control quickly and can result in you feeling unmotivated to cook.

Get really familiar with what you have in your fridge by giving it a thorough clean. Remove and dispose of any spoiled items, wipe down each of the fridge shelves or use warm soapy water to wash drawers. Return your items to the fridge in categories (use baskets if you need to). Having a space dedicated to one or more of the below categories may be helpful:

Condiments (jams, sauces, curry pastes)

Dairy (cheeses, yoghurt, cream, sour cream, butter)

Fruit and vegetables

Leftovers (labelled and dated)

Meal prep (items you have prepared ahead – see page 14)

Proteins (tofu, chicken, beef, pork, lamb, seafood)

 Hot tip
Group your spices together so you can easily find what you need and restock staples when they run low.

Hot tip

Keep a basket dedicated to refills of frequently used pantry items so you can replenish your canisters as they get low. Having a dedicated space helps prevent over-buying and duplicate purchases.

Once you have deep-cleaned and categorised your fridge, revisit it weekly (when you do your meal planning inventory – check page 11). It gives you the opportunity to give your shelves a quick wipe down if needed and will mean deep cleaning is required a lot less often (I normally use warm soapy water to wash the fridge drawers and shelves once every 4 months).

A clear fridge will make meal-planning easier (see page 16) because you will be able to see what you have at a glance. It will mean leftovers are eaten, you will reduce waste (no more half-opened unused jars, or veggies wilting and being thrown away) and, most importantly, it will make the overall experience of cooking more enjoyable.

Pantry

Your pantry, big or small, is the key to cooking efficiently. It can be frustrating wasting time and energy hunting for things you need when you are cooking. The key to having a pantry that stays organised is creating categories for your food, so you know where to find it and storing open foods in airtight containers and reusable sandwich bags to avoid spoilage.

If you feel your pantry needs an overhaul, start by removing all the items and disposing of those that have expired. Give the shelves a wipe down and return the items in categories, using baskets and turntables where practical. Once you have this system in place, it will be easy to revisit your pantry weekly as a part of your meal planning inventory check (see page 11) and ensure that you are using your ingredients versus landing with out-of-date food packets.

Once you have given the pantry a deep clean, you'll be revisiting it weekly as a part of your meal planning inventory check (see page 11), which will stop it from becoming cluttered with unusable ingredients again.

Category examples are:

Baking

Canned items

Noodles

Pasta

Sauces

Snacks

Keep it simple. Place frequently used items, such as snacks, sauces and canned items, at eye level. Put the items that you do not require on a daily basis on the top shelf, for example speciality baking items or items like napkins, party supplies or serving supplies.

Use airtight, labelled, clear containers to store opened flour, rice, breadcrumbs, dried legumes, nuts, snacks etc. to avoid duplicate purchases and stale items. Use a whiteboard marker or liquid chalk marker to record use-by dates on the base of your containers.

Other useful things to know

Freezer hacks

Store **sliced sourdough bread** in the freezer, ready to toast from frozen as needed.

Freeze **peeled ginger**, ready to grate on demand.

Freeze **ginger peel**, ready for ginger tea. Steep in boiling water for 2 minutes (just add honey and lemon).

Freeze **grated cheese** in reusable sandwich bags or airtight containers for up to 4 weeks. Thaw overnight in the fridge before using.

Freeze **left-over rice** in reusable sandwich bags or airtight containers for up to 2 months, then reheat until piping hot in the microwave.

Avoid half-opened pasta packets in the pantry. If a recipe calls for 250 g pasta, I make the whole 500 g bag, freeze the left-over cooked pasta and reheat it in the microwave, ready for another meal when I need it. Your Italian friends would never know it was frozen.

Make friends with the microwave

Whether you are adding pappadums directly to the turntable (1 minute and you can have crunchy, perfect pappadums), steaming perfectly cooked corn in its husk (page 194) or making sweet potato mash (page 28), the microwave has you covered and will help you speed through mealtimes effortlessly.

Shortcuts are okay

Frozen vegetables that are cut and ready and quality ready-made curry pastes or pasta sauces are all great options to help create delicious, affordable meals without spending hours in the kitchen.

Seasoning matters

Freshly ground black pepper and sea salt flakes have an incredible flavour profile and texture that will elevate your cooking. The recipes in this book use these and they are well worth the investment.

Grated cheese

Freshly grating your own cheese allows it to melt more smoothly as it doesn't contain the additives and thickening agents that many pre-grated cheeses from the supermarket do. It's also generally better value and tastes so much better, too!

Pan. Speedy stove-top meals to make weeknights a breeze

One-pan ginger–shallot chicken & rice

PREP TIME: 5 minutes

COOK TIME: 30 minutes

SERVES: 4

Note 1

Skin-on chicken thigh fillets are great, as the skin brings a deeper level of flavour to the dish, but skinless chicken thigh fillets can be used instead.

Note 2

A neutral-flavoured oil can be used if preferred, such as canola or vegetable oil.

Leftovers

Refrigerate for up to 3 days. Store the ginger and shallot oil separately. The olive oil will solidify, so allow it to come to room temperature before serving. Not suitable to freeze.

Hainanese chicken (poached chicken and fragrant rice cooked in chicken broth) is one of my family's favourite meals to eat and this is the one-pan, quick-and-easy version of that dish. It is perfect for those nights where I don't have a lot of time or energy as it has very minimal prep. The chicken and rice are perfectly cooked in the one pan with the simplest of ingredients (sea salt flakes, pepper and chicken stock – that's it!) and the star of the show is the ginger and shallot oil that you will want to put on everything. Teamed with a little drizzle of kecap manis (dark and sticky soy sauce), fresh sliced cucumbers and sambal oelek (chilli paste) for the adults, this is a meal you will want to make again and again.

5 large chicken thigh fillets
 (preferably skin on, see Note 1)
1 teaspoon sea salt flakes
½ teaspoon freshly ground
 black pepper
1 tablespoon olive oil
200 g (1 cup) jasmine or
 basmati rice
375 ml (1½ cups) chicken stock
kecap manis, to serve (optional)
sambal oelek or chilli oil, to serve
 (optional)
sliced cucumber and shredded
 spring onion, to serve

GINGER AND SHALLOT OIL

2 spring onions, finely sliced
1 teaspoon freshly grated ginger
½ teaspoon sea salt flakes
1 tablespoon sesame oil
80 ml (⅓ cup) olive oil (see Note 2)

Sprinkle the chicken with the salt and pepper.

Heat the olive oil in a large, heavy-based frying pan over medium–high heat and cook the chicken for 4–5 minutes or until golden, turning once halfway through cooking. Remove the chicken from the pan and set aside. Use a paper towel to drain excess fat if desired.

To the same pan, add the rice and stir for 30 seconds before adding the chicken stock. Bring to a simmer. Once the chicken stock is bubbling, return the chicken to the pan, cover, reduce the heat to the lowest setting and cook for 15 minutes.

For the ginger and shallot oil, combine the ingredients in a small bowl. Allow to stand while the chicken and rice cooks (the salt softens the spring onion and flavours the oil as it sits).

Once the chicken and rice are cooked, remove from the heat and allow to stand, covered, for 10 minutes.

Serve the chicken and rice topped with the ginger and shallot oil, kecap manis and sambal oelek or chilli oil (if using). Serve with the sliced cucumber and shredded spring onion on the side.

Coconut dal

Every once in a while I'll crave something that is vegetable-forward and warming from the inside out, and without fail I'll make a huge batch of this soothing coconut dal. I am a huge fan of lentils and legumes in general. They are inexpensive, easy to cook and can be flavoured with just about anything. The one thing that is even more awesome about the dried red lentils used in this recipe is that there is no soaking required. All the ingredients go directly into the pan and are cooked until soft and delicious before spinach and lemon juice are added to brighten the whole thing up. This dal is ideal for freezing, ready for quick lunches and easy dinners … and having a stash of store-bought roti in the freezer for dipping is a non-negotiable.

PREP TIME: 5 minutes

COOK TIME: 25 minutes

SERVES: 4

Note 1

You can freeze left-over canned tomatoes for up to 2 months in a reusable sandwich bag or airtight container, or try them in the Chicken Paprikash with Cabbage Salad on page 38.

Note 2

Opt for the soft and flaky roti in the freezer section of the supermarket. It heats in the pan just as you would find at your favourite local restaurant.

Leftovers

Refrigerate for up to 3 days. Freeze for up to 2 months.

Cook once, eat twice

Make fritters with left-over dal. Combine 250 g (1 cup) dal with 35 g (¼ cup) plain flour, 15 g (¼ cup) finely chopped coriander and 1 beaten egg. Add more flour if required to form four fritters. Cook for 2 minutes per side in 2 tablespoons of coconut oil in a large frying pan over medium heat. Serve with plain yoghurt and mango chutney.

375 g (1½ cups) dried red lentils
2 tablespoons coconut oil
1 onion, finely diced
1 tablespoon finely chopped garlic
1 tablespoon finely chopped ginger
1 teaspoon sweet paprika
1 teaspoon ground turmeric
1 teaspoon ground cumin
1 teaspoon garam masala
750 ml (3 cups) vegetable stock
250 ml (1 cup) coconut milk
200 g canned diced tomatoes
   (see Note 1)
1 teaspoon sea salt flakes
½ teaspoon freshly ground
   black pepper
1 tablespoon sugar
100 g (2 cups) baby spinach leaves
plain yoghurt, to serve
¼ bunch coriander, finely chopped,
   to serve
4 rotis, to serve (see Note 2)
lemon wedges, to serve

Place the lentils in a fine-mesh sieve and rinse under running water until the water runs clear.

Heat the coconut oil in a deep, heavy-based frying pan over medium heat. Add the onion and cook for 2–3 minutes until softened. Add the garlic and ginger and cook for a further 1 minute.

Add the spices and stir them through, then immediately add the rinsed lentils, vegetable stock, coconut milk, canned tomatoes, salt, pepper and sugar. Stir to combine, bring to a simmer and cook for 20 minutes, stirring occasionally, until the lentils have softened.

Add the spinach leaves and stir them through – as soon as they have wilted, remove the pan from the heat.

Serve with a swirl of plain yoghurt, some freshly chopped coriander, the flaky roti and a squeeze of lemon juice.

Chicken with creamy mushroom sauce

PREP TIME: 10 minutes

COOK TIME: 15 minutes

SERVES: 4

Leftovers

Refrigerate leftovers for up to 3 days. Not suitable to freeze.

Cook once, eat twice

Make a double batch of sauce to toss through your favourite pasta or stuff into baked potatoes.

This is the type of meal I used to order out in restaurants thinking there was no way I could replicate something so delicious in my own kitchen, let alone in under 30 minutes, at a fraction of the cost. But it turns out I absolutely can and now regularly do … with the help of my microwave. Yes. I know. The microwave. Washing up is an absolute breeze. Not only do I microwave my lemon and olive oil–tossed broccolini, but I also microwave whole sweet potatoes and they transform into the most perfect sweet potato mash to soak up all of that flavour-packed creamy mushroom sauce.

2 chicken breast fillets, cut in half horizontally to make 4 steaks
1 tablespoon plain flour
½ teaspoon sea salt flakes
½ teaspoon freshly ground black pepper
40 g unsalted butter
200 g mushrooms, sliced
1 tablespoon finely chopped garlic
1 teaspoon chicken stock powder

250 ml (1 cup) thickened cream
100 g (1 cup) freshly grated parmesan
Sweet Potato Mash, to serve (see Note 1)
Steamed Broccolini, to serve (see Note 2)
1 tablespoon finely chopped flat-leaf parsley, to serve

Sprinkle the chicken steaks with the flour, salt and pepper. Use your hands to coat the chicken evenly.

Heat 20 g of the butter in a large frying pan over medium heat. Add the chicken and cook for 2–3 minutes on each side until the chicken is golden and just cooked through. Remove the chicken from the pan and set aside on a plate.

Add 2–3 tablespoons of water to the pan to loosen up any sticky bits and stop them from burning. Add the remaining butter and the mushrooms and cook for 2–3 minutes until softened.

Add the garlic to the pan and cook, stirring, for 30 seconds. Add 80 ml (⅓ cup) of water, the chicken stock powder and cream. Bring to a gentle simmer and cook for 2 minutes or until the sauce has thickened slightly.

Stir through the parmesan, then return the chicken to the pan and let it cook for 1 minute. Serve with the sweet potato mash and steamed broccolini, with a sprinkling of parsley on top.

Note 1

Sweet potato mash
Add 2–3 sweet potatoes to a microwave-safe dish and prick them all over with a fork. Add 3 tablespoons water and microwave for 10–15 minutes on High, turning once halfway through cooking. When cooked, the sweet potato should be soft enough to be easily pierced with a fork. If it's still too firm, cook for longer in 3–5-minute intervals. Cut through the skin and scoop out the flesh using a spoon. Mash with a fork, sprinkle with sea salt flakes and freshly ground black pepper, drizzle with olive oil and serve.

Note 2

Steamed broccolini
Add 1 bunch of broccolini to a microwave-safe container. Add 3 tablespoons water and microwave on High, covered with the lid ajar, for 3–4 minutes (cook in 2-minute intervals until done to your liking). Drain and toss with olive oil, a squeeze of lemon juice, sea salt flakes and freshly ground black pepper.

Potato, leek & chorizo stew

PREP TIME: 10 minutes

COOK TIME: 1 hour

SERVES: 4

Note

Use two-thirds of the leek, including the pale green parts – just not the dark green top third, which can be too tough and fibrous to eat. Cut the leek into 2 cm chunks, then rinse it well under running water to remove any debris caught in the outer layers.

Leftovers

Refrigerate for up to 3 days. Freeze for up to 2 months. Thaw completely in the fridge overnight before reheating.

My mum makes a dish called poriluk, a stew made with thick pieces of leek, tender potato and smoked meats. When I asked for the recipe I discovered that the 'right' smoked meats are almost impossible to access unless you are, of course, my mum, who makes multiple trips to various butchers and delicatessens around Sydney for the best-quality, best-value produce. She has always been so considered with her purchases, which is something that has stuck with me. I found the best substitute for the smoked meats to be chorizo as it has the intensity needed. Don't be tempted to cut the leeks into small slices, as the rough, rustic chunks absorb all the incredible flavour. This is the type of soup you could happily eat multiple days in a row, especially with some crusty sourdough bread with butter (lots!) for soaking up all the goodness.

1 tablespoon olive oil
300 g chorizo (roughly 3 chorizo sausages), cut into bite-sized rounds
2 large leeks, cut into thick slices (see Note)
6 potatoes, peeled and cut into bite-sized pieces
2 tablespoons plain flour
1 tablespoon sweet paprika
2 teaspoons chicken stock powder
2 bay leaves
1 teaspoon sea salt flakes
½ teaspoon freshly ground black pepper
crusty sourdough bread and butter, to serve

Heat the olive oil in a large stockpot over medium–high heat. Add the chorizo and cook, stirring, for 5–8 minutes until the chorizo begins to turn golden and release its oils.

Add the leek and potato to the pot and cook, stirring, for 2 minutes.

Add the flour and paprika to the pot and stir them through. Add 250 ml (1 cup) water and use a whisk to combine it as much as possible with the ingredients in the pan. Add 1.75 litres water, the chicken stock powder, bay leaves, salt and pepper. Bring to the boil, then reduce the heat to the lowest setting. Cover with a lid slightly ajar and cook for 45 minutes or until the potatoes and leek have softened. Serve with the crusty bread and lashings of butter.

Lamb kofta with fattoush salad & hummus

PREP TIME: 30 minutes

COOK TIME: 40 minutes

SERVES: 4

Leftovers

Kofta Cooked kofta can be refrigerated for up to 3 days.

Fattoush Best prepared and eaten immediately.

Hummus Refrigerate for up to 3 days.

Pita crisps Store in an airtight container for up to 3 days (delicious dipped in the hummus).

Make ahead

Fattoush See the food storage tips on page 15 for how to prepare your salad ingredients in advance.

Kofta Prepare as per the recipe and freeze, uncooked, in an airtight container with baking paper between the layers to stop the kofta sticking. Thaw completely in the fridge overnight before cooking.

Cook once, eat twice

Try the fattoush with the falafels on page 41. Make lamb wraps by stuffing the kofta into wraps with the tabbouleh on page 41.

Last summer one of our friends came over for lunch and made lamb kebabs for us – a recipe that had been passed down to him from his grandfather. What an absolute treat! These lamb koftas are like nothing I've tried before. The spice mixture is simple yet an absolute flavour bomb, especially when served with fattoush salad and hummus. Don't feel limited to lamb – these are also delicious made with beef mince, and the salad ingredients can be modified to whatever is in season. I always make a few extra kofta for the freezer so I've got a quick dinner up my sleeve if I need it. Our friend would be disappointed to not see rice included in this recipe, so some medium-grain rice cooked in chicken stock with a few blobs of butter is a nice little side to enjoy with this, especially when stuffed into pita bread. Skip the premade store-bought koftas and give these a go. You won't look back.

FATTOUSH

Pita crisps
1 pita bread
2 tablespoons olive oil
1 teaspoon sea salt flakes

Dressing
80 ml (⅓ cup) olive oil
2 tablespoons freshly squeezed
  lemon juice
1 teaspoon sea salt flakes
½ teaspoon dried mint
½ teaspoon sumac
½ teaspoon freshly ground
  black pepper

Salad
1 large or 2 small gem lettuces,
  cut into bite-sized pieces
250 g cherry tomatoes, halved
80 g (½ cup) diced capsicum
2 Lebanese cucumbers, sliced
5 radishes, sliced
¼ red onion, sliced
½ bunch flat-leaf parsley,
  roughly chopped
1 tablespoon pomegranate seeds
  (optional)

HUMMUS

400 g can chickpeas, rinsed
  and drained
½ teaspoon bicarbonate of soda
2 tablespoons tahini
½ teaspoon freshly grated garlic
3 tablespoons freshly squeezed
  lemon juice
1 teaspoon sea salt flakes
2 tablespoons olive oil
2 tablespoons ice-cold water

LAMB KOFTA

8 wooden skewers
500 g lamb mince
1 teaspoon freshly grated garlic
2 tablespoons finely chopped
  mint leaves
1 onion, grated
2 teaspoons ground cumin
2 teaspoons sweet paprika
1 teaspoon ground coriander
½ teaspoon ground turmeric
½ teaspoon bicarbonate of soda
1½ teaspoons sea salt flakes
½ teaspoon freshly ground
  black pepper
3 tablespoons olive oil
lemon wedges, to serve

Start by making the fattoush. Preheat the oven to 200°C fan-forced.

For the pita crisps, brush (or spray) the pita bread with the olive oil and sprinkle it with salt. Bake for 8–10 minutes until crisp and golden, turning halfway through cooking. Use your hands to break the pita into shards.

For the dressing, whisk all the ingredients in a small bowl to combine.

For the salad, arrange the ingredients in a large serving bowl, topping with the parsley and pomegranate seeds (if using) last. Drizzle with the dressing and top with the pita shards.

For the hummus, place the chickpeas and bicarbonate of soda in a small saucepan and add water to cover by at least 2 cm. Bring to a simmer, then cook, covered, for 20 minutes on the lowest heat setting, until the chickpeas are soft and the skins are falling off. Drain in a fine-mesh sieve and rinse under cold tap water for 30 seconds.

Place the tahini, garlic, lemon juice and salt in a food processor and blend for 1 minute until smooth and creamy.

Add the cooked, drained chickpeas and blend for 2 minutes. With the food processor running, add the olive oil gradually until combined – stop and scrape down the side of the food processor as needed.

Add 1–2 tablespoons of ice-cold water and stir until you have a smooth, pale consistency.

For the kofta, soak the skewers in water for a minimum of 5 minutes. Combine all the kofta ingredients, except the olive oil and lemon wedges, in a large bowl and mix well with your hands.

Divide the kofta mixture into eight portions, then form them into sausage shapes on the skewers. Fill a small bowl with tap water to wet your hands as you make the kofta, to prevent the kofta mixture sticking.

Heat 1 tablespoon of olive oil in a large frying pan over medium–high heat and cook the kofta in batches for 8–10 minutes, turning regularly until browned all over and cooked through, and adding more oil as needed.

Serve the kofta, fattoush and hummus in the centre of the table for everyone to help themselves.

Easy butter chicken

PREP TIME: 10 minutes

COOK TIME: 15 minutes

SERVES: 4

Leftovers

Refrigerate for up to 3 days or freeze for up to 2 months. Thaw in the fridge overnight before reheating.

Cook once, eat twice

Double the recipe and make butter chicken pot pies! Divide 370 g (2 cups) cooked rice between four oven-proof ramekins. Top the rice with the butter chicken mixture, top with store-bought puff pastry and brush the pastry all over with whisked egg. Bake in a 200°C fan-forced oven for 20 minutes or until the pastry is golden and crispy.

I purchased butter chicken simmer sauce sachets for years when I needed extra-easy dinners for busy days. But aside from not being the best value (those sauces can be expensive), I found that they just didn't taste as good as the real thing. I attempted to make butter chicken from scratch multiple times, but found recipes to be complex with long marinating times or needing a food processor … and I draw the line at using my food processor on weeknights! I'd just about given up with experimenting when I finally came up with the best, easiest butter chicken recipe made with the simplest of ingredients. The flavour is intense and delicious and the entire dish is on the table in less than 30 minutes – with minimal clean-up.

1 tablespoon olive oil
20 g unsalted butter
1 onion, finely diced
2 garlic cloves, finely chopped
1 tablespoon finely chopped or grated ginger
500 g chicken thigh fillets, cut into bite-sized pieces
2 teaspoons garam masala
1 teaspoon ground cumin
1 teaspoon yellow mustard seeds
1 teaspoon ground turmeric
1 teaspoon sea salt flakes
¼ teaspoon freshly ground black pepper
2 tablespoons tomato paste
250 ml (1 cup) thickened cream

TO SERVE
2 tablespoons plain yoghurt
1 Lebanese cucumber, finely sliced
½ red onion, finely sliced
¼ bunch coriander, leaves picked
pappadums
steamed basmati rice, topped with fried shallots (optional)
2 bird's eye chillies (optional)

Heat the olive oil and butter in a large frying pan over medium–high heat. Add the onion, garlic and ginger. Cook, stirring, for 1 minute until fragrant.

Add the chicken, garam masala, cumin, yellow mustard seeds, turmeric, salt and pepper. Cook, stirring, for 2–3 minutes until the chicken is slightly browned.

Add the tomato paste and cream and stir them through. Simmer over medium–low heat, uncovered, for 8 minutes or until the chicken is cooked.

Serve with the yoghurt, cucumber, red onion, coriander leaves, pappadums and steamed basmati rice. Top with the chillies, if desired.

Chicken paprikash with cabbage salad

PREP TIME: 10 minutes

COOK TIME: 55 minutes

SERVES: 4–6

Note

You can freeze left-over canned crushed tomatoes for up to 2 months in a reusable sandwich bag or airtight container.

Leftovers

Refrigerate for up to 3 days or freeze for up to 3 months. Thaw completely in the fridge overnight before reheating.

Cook once, eat twice

Don't throw out that left-over cabbage salad! Serve it with chicken schnitzel (page 74) and Creamy Potato Salad (page 120) – they are a match made in heaven. Try cevapcici (skinless beef sausages), cabbage salad, sliced red onion and ajvar (capsicum relish) on a roll for the ultimate sandwich experience. Cevapcici and ajvar can be found at most major supermarkets or at continental delicatessens.

My husband has a rating system for all my recipes and this meal received a 9/10. For the record, this is the highest score he has ever given any of my dishes. I know … and he's a tough critic. This is the type of meal that soothes my soul. It's another dish I grew up eating. It's packed with flavour, it's very easy to make with fall-off-the-bone chicken and is ready to devour in less than an hour. The chicken is simmered in a tomato and capsicum gravy, which is finished with a dollop of sour cream for extra richness. You can serve it with pasta, rice, bread, mashed potatoes or polenta (page 148). The cabbage salad I serve with this meal is famous in my parents' hometown and is now famous at my place too – the kids love it!

1.2 kg chicken drumsticks and
    bone-in chicken thigh cutlets
2 teaspoons sea salt flakes
1 teaspoon freshly ground
    black pepper
2 tablespoons plain flour
2 tablespoons olive oil
40 g unsalted butter
2 large onions, finely diced
1 red capsicum, finely sliced
1 teaspoon freshly grated garlic
2 tablespoons tomato paste
2 tablespoons sweet paprika
500 ml (2 cups) chicken stock
200 g canned crushed tomatoes
    (see Note)

1 teaspoon sugar
2 tablespoons sour cream
1 tablespoon finely chopped
    flat-leaf parsley (optional)
pasta of choice, to serve

CABBAGE SALAD
300 g (4 cups) finely sliced
    green cabbage
80 ml (⅓ cup) olive oil
2 tablespoons apple cider vinegar
1 teaspoon sea salt flakes
¼ teaspoon freshly ground
    black pepper

To make the cabbage salad, combine the ingredients in a large bowl and toss well.

Season the chicken with half the salt and pepper and dust all over with the flour. Heat the olive oil in a large, heavy-based frying pan over medium–high heat and cook the chicken in batches for 2–3 minutes until browned all over. Remove the chicken from the pan and set aside on a plate.

Add the butter to the same pan and, once melted, add the onion and cook, stirring, for 2–3 minutes until softened. Add the capsicum and garlic and cook, stirring, for a further 2 minutes. Add the tomato paste and paprika and stir them through, then immediately add the chicken stock, crushed tomatoes, the remaining salt and pepper and the sugar. Return the chicken to the pan and bring to the boil before reducing the heat to medium–low. Cover and simmer for 40 minutes, stirring once halfway through cooking.

Remove the chicken from the pan and place it in a shallow dish.

Mix the sour cream into the sauce, then pour it over the chicken. Sprinkle with the parsley (if using) and serve with the cabbage salad and pasta.

Homemade falafels with cheat's tabbouleh

PREP TIME: 20 minutes

COOK TIME: 15 minutes

MAKES: 16

If you've only ever eaten falafels in a snack pack from your local kebab shop (which absolutely has its time and place), prepare to be wowed. I only started making these in recent years when I finally got myself a food processor (now, arguably, one of my most used appliances, second in line to the toaster and coffee machine). But if you don't have a food processor, never fear, as you can even make these in a blender using the pulse setting. Stuffed into little pita breads with a cheat's tabbouleh (no cracked wheat – no problem!) and drizzled with hummus, these are the perfect lunch or dinner option. Admittedly, the kids still aren't completely on board with these yet, but that's okay. I freeze a whole batch and it is so great to have something to lean into on those busier days when I need something fast for lunch.

Note

Vegetable oil, canola oil or sunflower oil will produce the crispiest results. The oil needs to be at least 2 cm deep with the falafels completely submerged.

Leftovers

Refrigerate for up to 3 days in an airtight container. Eat the falafels cold or reheat them in the microwave (not the oven as it will dry them out). Freeze for up to 4 weeks. Refrigerate the tabbouleh (undressed) in an airtight container for up to 2 days. Drizzle with the dressing just before serving.

Cook once, eat twice

Use leftovers to make falafel bowls. Top brown rice with the falafels, tabbouleh, canned chickpeas, diced tomatoes, sliced cucumber and sliced red onion, spinach leaves, feta, olives and hummus.

220 g (1 cup) dried chickpeas
¼ teaspoon bicarbonate of soda
1 teaspoon freshly grated garlic
½ bunch flat-leaf parsley, roughly chopped
½ bunch coriander, roughly chopped
4 spring onions, roughly chopped
1 teaspoon ground coriander
1 teaspoon ground cumin
1 teaspoon sea salt flakes
½ teaspoon freshly ground black pepper
½ teaspoon baking powder
2 tablespoons plain flour
oil, for frying (see Note)

CHEAT'S TABBOULEH
1 bunch flat-leaf parsley, roughly chopped
½ bunch mint, leaves picked and roughly chopped
2 tomatoes, finely diced
1 spring onion, sliced
2 tablespoons freshly squeezed lemon juice
2 tablespoons olive oil
1 teaspoon sea salt flakes

TO SERVE
4 pita bread pockets
110 g (½ cup) store-bought or homemade hummus (page 32)
lemon wedges

Combine the dried chickpeas with the bicarbonate of soda in a deep bowl and cover with cold water. Soak overnight (18–24 hours). Rinse and drain.

Add the chickpeas, garlic, parsley, coriander, spring onion, ground coriander, cumin, salt, pepper, baking powder and flour to a food processor and process for at least 3 minutes until finely chopped. Refrigerate for at least 1 hour.

Scoop tablespoons (or ice-cream scoops) of the mixture and shape into patties, roughly golf ball–sized and flattened so the inside cooks evenly. Wet your hands regularly to stop the mixture sticking to your fingers. Cook the falafels immediately once rolled.

Heat the oil in a large, deep frying pan over medium heat (don't heat the oil over high heat or the falafels will brown too quickly on the outside) and fry the falafels in batches for 3–4 minutes until golden and crisp.

Prepare the cheat's tabbouleh by combining the ingredients in a bowl.

Serve the falafels and tabbouleh with the pita bread pockets, hummus and lemon wedges.

Crispy sesame chicken

PREP TIME: 10 minutes

COOK TIME: 10 minutes

SERVES: 4

Note

Use a high smoke-point oil like canola, sunflower or vegetable oil, which will produce the crispiest results. The oil needs to be at least 1 cm deep. Olive oil can be used to shallow-fry, but the chicken will need to be cooked for longer (3–4 minutes more) and the results may not be as crispy.

Leftovers

Refrigerate for up to 3 days in an airtight container. The chicken will soften but will be equally delicious. Not suitable to freeze.

As a family we make a conscious effort to prepare most of our meals at home. I get huge satisfaction from saving money and knowing exactly what is going into our food. This recipe very quickly went viral on my social media accounts, being viewed more than 11 million times. It is delicious, yet made with the simplest of ingredients. Every time I make this, there are at least two family members hovering behind me asking 'when will dinner be ready?'. Lucky for them (and me), this is a super-quick meal to prepare, on the table in less than 20 minutes, making it perfect for busy weeknights or relaxed weekends.

500 g chicken thigh fillets, cut into 1–2 cm strips (can be substituted with chicken breast)
1 egg, whisked
1 teaspoon garlic powder
1 teaspoon sweet paprika
½ teaspoon sea salt flakes
½ teaspoon freshly ground black pepper
60 g (½ cup) cornflour
oil, for frying (see Note)
1 spring onion, finely sliced, to serve
1 teaspoon toasted sesame seeds, to serve
steamed rice, to serve

SAUCE
1 teaspoon finely chopped garlic
3 tablespoons tamari or soy sauce
45 g (¼ cup) brown sugar
1 teaspoon sesame oil
1 tablespoon olive oil
1 tablespoon cornflour mixed with 125 ml (½ cup) water

In a large bowl, combine the chicken, egg, garlic powder, paprika, salt, pepper and cornflour. Mix to coat the chicken well – the ingredients will form a thick paste around the chicken.

Heat the oil in a large, deep saucepan over medium–high heat and fry the chicken for 3–4 minutes until golden. Set the chicken aside to drain on a plate lined with paper towel.

For the sauce, in a small bowl, combine the garlic, tamari or soy sauce, brown sugar, sesame oil and olive oil.

Heat a large frying pan over medium–low heat and add the sauce. Allow it to simmer for 2–3 minutes or until thickened.

Add the cornflour and water mixture. Increase the heat to medium–high and simmer for a further 2–3 minutes until the sauce is glossy. If the sauce is too thick, add 1 tablespoon of water at a time until it is the consistency of honey.

Remove the pan from the heat. Return the chicken to the pan and stir to coat it in the sauce.

Top with the spring onion and sesame seeds. Serve with the steamed rice, or make it a full banquet with Classic Fried Rice (page 99) and Homemade Crisp-fried Pork Spring Rolls (page 187).

Bakes. Delicious fuss-free dishes to whack straight in the oven

Cheesy potato gratin

PREP TIME: 15 minutes

COOK TIME: 1 hour
30 minutes

SERVES: 6–8

Note

Use a sharp knife to slice
the potatoes (slice them
as finely as possible,
aiming for 3 mm thick),
or use a mandoline or
food processor with
the slicing attachment.

Hot tip

Potato gratin makes the
perfect side for roast
chicken (page 54). Both
recipes are cooked at 180°C
fan-forced so they can be
prepared simultaneously.
Place the chicken on
the top rack of the oven
and the gratin on the
bottom rack.

Leftovers

Refrigerate in an airtight
container for up to 3 days.
Reheat in the oven or
microwave.

Make ahead

Cook as per the recipe,
cover with foil and
refrigerate up to 48 hours
before you need it. Cover
and reheat in a 180°C fan-
forced oven for 45 minutes
or until warmed through.

We celebrate special occasions like birthdays with our immediate family and
it's normally a barbecue with a whole heap of side dishes. I have been making
this potato gratin for years and I have learned that 'mixing it up' and 'making
something different' is never the answer. We all love this gratin so much that
I now make two trays. It has such a wow factor, especially with the vertical
placement of the potatoes, which allows for a super-crispy, golden top and
a soft and creamy bottom. It's so luxurious yet so easy to make, with simple
ingredients, and can be prepared ahead of time, ready for when you need to
serve a crowd.

1.5 kg potatoes, any variety, peeled
   and finely sliced (see Note)
40 g unsalted butter, melted
500 ml (2 cups) thickened cream
1 tablespoon finely chopped garlic

2 teaspoons sea salt flakes
1 teaspoon chicken stock powder
2 thyme sprigs, leaves picked
125 g (1 cup) freshly grated
   tasty cheese

Preheat the oven to 180°C fan-forced.

In a medium baking dish, arrange the potato slices vertically so they are
firmly packed.

Combine the melted butter, thickened cream, garlic, salt and stock powder in
a jug, then pour the mixture over the potato. Sprinkle with the thyme leaves,
followed by the cheese. Place the dish on a baking tray in case of any overflow.

Cover with baking paper (to stop the cheese sticking), then foil, and bake for
1 hour and 15 minutes or until the potato is tender and can be easily pierced
with a fork.

Remove the foil and baking paper and cook the potato under the oven grill for
15 minutes or until golden (this will happen quickly so keep an eye on it to stop
it burning). Let the gratin stand for 10 minutes to absorb any remaining liquid
before serving.

Sticky soy chicken wings

PREP TIME: 10 minutes

COOK TIME: 1 hour

SERVES: 4

Leftovers

Refrigerate the cooked chicken wings for up to 3 days.

Make ahead

Marinate the chicken wings as per the recipe and freeze them, uncooked, in an airtight container for up to 2 months. Thaw completely in the fridge overnight, then cook as per the recipe.

If I was to pick my top five meals, this would be one of them. Huge call, but these fall-off-the-bone, sticky soy chicken wings are so moreish and delicious, but they're fuss-free and inexpensive to make. The marinade is made with simple supermarket ingredients, yet you are left with an incredible depth of flavour that pairs so well with the freshness of the cucumber and ginger salad. The chicken wings can be marinated and frozen for when you need them. And the best part? It's a meal just made for eating in front of the TV, on the lounge, in pyjamas.

1 kg chicken wings, cut into drumettes and wingettes
1 teaspoon white sesame seeds, to sprinkle (optional)
1 spring onion, finely sliced (optional)
1 bird's eye chilli, sliced (optional)
steamed jasmine rice, to serve

CUCUMBER AND GINGER SALAD
1 tablespoon rice wine vinegar
1 tablespoon chilli oil (optional)
1 teaspoon caster sugar
1 teaspoon sea salt flakes
1 teaspoon finely chopped ginger
1 tablespoon sesame oil
2 Lebanese cucumbers, sliced

MARINADE
3 tablespoons ketchup
3 tablespoons tamari or soy sauce
1 tablespoon dark soy sauce
1 tablespoon sesame oil
1 tablespoon rice wine vinegar (or white vinegar)
1 tablespoon finely chopped garlic

Combine the cucumber and ginger salad ingredients in a bowl and set aside.

Combine the marinade ingredients in a bowl and set aside.

Preheat the oven to 180°C fan-forced.

Place the chicken in a baking dish that is large enough so that the chicken pieces are not overlapping. Add the marinade to the dish and use your hands to ensure the chicken is evenly coated.

Bake for 1 hour, turning the chicken halfway through cooking and adding 3 tablespoons of water to the base of the pan and shuffling the chicken to loosen any sticky bits.

Allow the chicken to rest for at least 10 minutes before serving. Sprinkle the chicken wings with the sesame seeds, spring onion and chilli (if using).

Serve with the steamed rice and the cucumber and ginger salad, or enjoy with creamy coleslaw (page 139).

Pepperoni & zucchini pizza

PREP TIME: 10 minutes

COOK TIME: 22 minutes

SERVES: 4

Leftovers

Refrigerate left-over cooked pizza for up to 2 days. Reheat or eat it cold (perfect for lunch boxes). Freeze for up to 2 months. Thaw completely in the fridge before reheating to stop the base drying out.

When I made this pizza dough for the first time a few years ago, I was floored. Imagine homemade pizza dough but with no waiting, no proving and no rolling. And the best part? Two-ingredient dough, which is perfectly cooked and outrageously fluffy. There are some extra tips in the recipe that can be applied to all pizzas, even if you are using store-bought pizza bases. The golden rule is dough, sauce, cheese and then toppings. This allows the cheese to get gloriously melty while the toppings crisp up and caramelise. Another tip is to combine a little freshly grated garlic with olive oil and sea salt flakes to drizzle on the pizza before baking. Life changing.

260 g (1¾ cups) self-raising flour, plus extra for dusting
250 g (1 cup) plain Greek yoghurt
60 g (¼ cup) tomato paste
150 g (1 cup) freshly grated mozzarella
50 g pepperoni, finely sliced
1 zucchini, shaved into ribbons using a vegetable peeler

100 g grape tomatoes, halved
½ teaspoon freshly grated garlic
2 tablespoons olive oil, plus an extra 1 tablespoon or olive oil spray to brush
½ teaspoon sea salt flakes

Preheat the oven to 200°C fan-forced.

In a large bowl, mix together the flour and yoghurt until they form a ball. If the dough resembles large flakes and doesn't seem to be binding, use your hands to knead it a couple of times so that the flour and yoghurt are completely combined. Use extra flour on your hands and on the dough to stop your hands sticking.

Line a baking tray with baking paper. Sprinkle it with a little extra flour and place the dough ball in the centre. Use your hands to press the dough ball into a flat shape – it can be oval, round or square. The easiest way to do this is by using your fists and knuckles to gently pound and stretch the dough into shape. Aim for a 1 cm thickness but it doesn't need to be perfect. Flip the dough over as you shape it as needed, to stop it from sticking to the baking paper. Sprinkle on more flour if the dough is starting to stick.

Top the dough with the tomato paste and cheese. Add the pepperoni, zucchini and grape tomatoes.

In a small bowl, combine the garlic, olive oil and salt. Drizzle the mixture over the pizza, paying particular attention to the grape tomatoes. This will give the pizza an extra depth of flavour. Spray (or brush) the crusts of the pizza generously with olive oil to ensure they turn golden. Bake for 20–22 minutes.

Serve with a simple green salad. Try the caesar dressing on page 126 or the balsamic dressing on page 70.

Spanakopita 'greens' pie

PREP TIME: 10 minutes

COOK TIME: 30 minutes

SERVES: 4

Note

Thaw the spinach as per the packet instructions and drain through a fine-mesh sieve. Wrap the spinach in a damp, clean tea towel and use your hands to wring out any excess water. The drier the spinach, the crispier the pastry.

Leftovers

Refrigerate cooked spanakopita for up to 3 days. Freeze in individual portions for up to 4 weeks. Reheat in a 180°C fan-forced oven. It can be eaten cold too, and leftovers make great lunch box fillers.

Make ahead

The pie can be assembled and refrigerated up to 24 hours prior to baking, or frozen for up to 4 weeks. Bake from frozen in a 180°C fan-forced oven (allow up to an hour).

Many moons ago my husband and I honeymooned in Greece and I'm not overexaggerating when I say I ate a piece of spanakopita every single day in between lounging on sun chairs, riding around on quad bikes (terrifying) and fish pedicure spa experiences (equally terrifying). I pined for spanakopita for years before realising how easy it is to make. There's hardly any chopping or fussing; you just mix it all up and into the oven it goes. Filo pastry used to scare me, but it's one of the easiest pastries to work with and is found at most supermarkets. The flavour combination here is incredible and the kids love it too, even though I watch them with horror as they squeeze ketchup all over their serves.

750 g frozen spinach, thawed and drained well (see Note)
6 spring onions, finely sliced
½ bunch dill, fronds picked and finely chopped
½ bunch mint, leaves picked and finely chopped
4 eggs

300 g fresh ricotta
200 g feta, crumbled
1 teaspoon sea salt flakes
¼ teaspoon freshly ground black pepper
8–10 sheets filo pastry
olive oil spray
black sesame seeds, to sprinkle

Preheat the oven to 200°C fan-forced.

In a large bowl, use your hands to combine the frozen spinach, spring onion, dill, mint, eggs, ricotta, feta, salt and pepper.

Layer four sheets of filo pastry in a baking dish, spraying or brushing with olive oil between each layer. There will be some overhang.

Place the spinach mixture into the baking dish, folding the overhanging filo pastry back onto the mixture. Scrunch the remaining sheets of filo into rough balls and place them on top of the pie, spraying with olive oil. Sprinkle with the black sesame seeds.

Bake for 30 minutes in the bottom half of the oven (to ensure a crispy base) until the pastry is golden brown. Allow to stand for 10 minutes before serving. Serve warm or at room temperature.

Roast chicken with ultimate roasted potatoes

PREP TIME: 20 minutes

COOK TIME: 1 hour 45 minutes

SERVES: 4

Note

For a quick dinner, trussing with twine isn't necessary. The idea behind trussing is that the twine assists in sealing in juices and allows the chicken to cook more evenly. I have made this recipe hundreds of times and, other than for the sake of presentation, there is never any significant difference in flavour, so feel free to skip this step.

Leftovers

Refrigerate left-over chicken and gravy for up to 3 days. Refrigerate left-over potatoes for up to 3 days and reheat them in the oven to retain their crunch.

Make ahead

Marinate and refrigerate the chicken for up to 48 hours before cooking. The potatoes can also be peeled and cut, submerged in cold tap water and refrigerated for up to 24 hours prior to cooking. When ready to use, drain the potatoes and use them as per the recipe.

On the first day of my son starting school, I tenderly got myself home after dropping him off and immediately started preparing this meal for him to enjoy when he got home. In actual fact, it was more of an attempt to comfort myself. I don't know how many chickens I roasted in the following weeks (lots!), but I do know that this roast chicken is one of our favourite meals to eat. You may have guessed that this is also one of our 'core meals' (see page 11 to learn more). There is no marinating of the chicken required, no stuffing anything under skin, and no other intimidating preparation before you can get this dish in the oven. The oven does all the hard work. The chicken is served with the ultimate roasted potatoes and a rich, nourishing, vegetable-filled gravy. The chicken and potatoes can be cooked simultaneously in the oven.

ROASTED POTATOES

1.2 kg potatoes (any variety), peeled and quartered (in eighths if large)
125 ml (½ cup) olive oil
2 tablespoons plain flour (this is the key to crispy potatoes!)
2 teaspoons sea salt flakes, plus extra to serve

ROASTING VEGETABLES

2 carrots, peeled and halved lengthways
2 brown or red onions, cut in half (or quarters if large)
1 whole garlic bulb, halved horizontally (leave the skin on)
2 tablespoons olive oil
½ teaspoon sea salt flakes
½ teaspoon freshly ground black pepper

CHICKEN

1 whole chicken (1.2–1.8 kg)
3 tablespoons olive oil
2 teaspoons sweet paprika
2 teaspoons dried herbs of choice (thyme or oregano work well)
1 teaspoon chicken stock powder (or sea salt flakes)
½ teaspoon freshly ground black pepper
2 thick slices lemon
cooking twine (optional, see Note)

GRAVY

2 tablespoons plain flour
500 ml (2 cups) chicken stock

TO SERVE

steamed green beans
thyme or oregano leaves (optional)

Cook once, eat twice

Left-over chicken Use left-over chicken in school lunch box sandwiches, salads (page 123), Peri-peri Chicken Burgers (page 178) or in rice paper rolls (page 193).

Left-over bones Keep left-over bones from the chicken to make a bone broth. Place the bones in a large pot along with 4 carrots, cut into 5 cm lengths; 2 onions, quartered; 4 celery stalks (leaves included); 4 litres water (or enough to cover the chicken bones and vegetables); 3 teaspoons sea salt flakes; and 1 tablespoon apple cider vinegar. Bring to the boil, then reduce the heat to the lowest setting. Simmer, covered, for at least 3–4 hours. Strain through a fine-mesh sieve and refrigerate for up to 3 days or freeze for up to 2 months. Use as a base for soups, stews and pastas. High in collagen, the broth will become gelatinous in the fridge but will liquify when reheated.

Preheat the oven to 180°C fan-forced. Preheat a large baking tray in the oven (it needs to be wide and deep enough to fit the potatoes without them overlapping).

Place the potatoes in a large saucepan and cover them with water (ensure there isn't too much water; the potatoes should be just submerged). Bring to the boil. Once the water starts to boil rapidly, turn the heat down to medium–low and simmer for 2 minutes.

While the potatoes are cooking, add the olive oil to the preheated baking tray in the oven (leave the tray in the oven so that the olive oil warms).

Drain the potatoes in a colander and shake them around to rough up the edges. Sprinkle the flour over the potatoes and stir to coat (the potatoes may break up a little, which is okay). Add the potatoes to the baking tray (the oil will be hot and will splatter, so be careful). Toss the potatoes, so they are evenly coated in the oil. Add the salt.

Meanwhile, place the carrot, onion, garlic, olive oil, salt and pepper on a large deep baking tray. Toss to coat. Place the chicken on top of the vegetables and pat dry with paper towel (this helps to crisp up the skin).

Drizzle the chicken with the olive oil and sprinkle with the paprika, dried herbs, chicken stock powder (or salt) and pepper. Use your hands to rub the spice mixture all over the chicken evenly. Stuff the two lemon slices into the cavity of the chicken and tie the legs together with the twine (if using, see Note).

Place the chicken on the top rack of your oven and the potatoes on the bottom rack.

Roast the potatoes for 1½ hours, turning them every 30 minutes.

Roast the chicken, uncovered, for 45 minutes, then add 125 ml (½ cup) water and shuffle the vegetables and chicken around to stop the vegetables from burning. Bake for a further 45 minutes.

Remove the roasted potatoes and chicken from the oven.

Sprinkle the roasted potatoes with the extra salt.

Set the chicken aside, loosely covered with foil, for at least 10 minutes to ensure it is succulent and soft. Leave the vegetables in the tray for the gravy.

For the gravy, place the baking tray with the vegetables on the stovetop over medium–high heat. If you don't have a baking tray compatible with your stovetop, transfer the vegetables and pan drippings to a large frying pan instead. Add the flour and cook, stirring, for 1 minute until a paste forms. Add the chicken stock and simmer for 2–3 minutes, occasionally stirring, until the gravy thickens. If the gravy is too thick, you can slowly add some water, 1 tablespoon at a time, until you achieve your desired consistency.

Strain the gravy through a fine-mesh sieve into a serving jug, pushing as much vegetable mix as possible through the sieve to create a thick gravy.

Serve the chicken, roasted potatoes and gravy with the steamed green beans and a sprinkling of thyme or oregano leaves (if using).

Nachos with quick guacamole & homemade salsa

PREP TIME: 10 minutes

COOK TIME: 15 minutes

SERVES: 4

Note 1

Quick guacamole
Mash 1 avocado with
1 tablespoon chopped
coriander, 1 tablespoon
freshly squeezed lime
juice and ½ teaspoon
sea salt flakes.

Note 2

Tomato salsa
Combine 1 large diced
tomato with half a diced
red onion, 1 tablespoon
chopped coriander,
1 tablespoon freshly
squeezed lime juice and
½ teaspoon sea salt flakes.

Leftovers

Refrigerate the beef mince
mixture for up to 3 days or
freeze for up to 2 months.
Thaw completely in the
fridge overnight before
reheating.

Cook once, eat twice

Make a double batch of
the beef mixture to serve
with rice and salad and
transform this meal into
beef burrito bowls.

These nachos are one of my 'core meals' (see page 11 to learn more), which
I know my family love and want to eat regularly. Having a collection of these
meals up your sleeve makes dinnertime a lot less stressful. The first time I made
the homemade nacho seasoning, I knew I'd never buy the store-bought variety
again. It's so fast and easy to prepare and is made with pantry staples. The
filling is freezer-friendly so you can make double to have a batch for when you
need it, and even repurpose it to create different meals – think burrito bowls
and quesadillas. And of course, to top it off, there is a quick guacamole
involved … which is basically my version of self-care.

1 tablespoon sweet paprika
1 tablespoon ground cumin
1 teaspoon onion powder
1 teaspoon dried oregano
1 teaspoon sea salt flakes
1 tablespoon olive oil
1 onion, finely diced
1 teaspoon finely chopped garlic
250 g beef mince
2 tablespoons tomato paste
400 g can kidney beans (or any
   beans, or substitute with another
   250 g beef mince), rinsed
   and drained
200 g corn chips
125 g (1 cup) freshly grated
   tasty cheese

TO SERVE
Quick Guacamole (see Note 1)
Tomato Salsa (see Note 2)
1 jalapeño, finely sliced
125 g (½ cup) sour cream

Preheat the oven grill to high.

Combine the paprika, cumin, onion powder, oregano and salt in a small bowl.

Heat the olive oil in a large frying pan over medium–high heat, add the onion
and garlic and cook for 1–2 minutes until softened.

Add the beef mince to the pan and cook for 3–4 minutes until browned, breaking
it up as you go. Add the mixed spices, tomato paste, kidney beans and
3 tablespoons water and cook for 2 minutes.

Arrange the corn chips in an oven-proof dish, then top them with the beef mixture
and the cheese. Grill for 2–4 minutes until golden and the cheese is melted.

Top with quick guacamole, tomato salsa and sliced jalapeño and serve with sour
cream on the side.

Roasted chicken with cabbage & bacon

PREP TIME: 10 minutes

COOK TIME: 1 hour

SERVES: 4

Make ahead

Shred the cabbage ready for when you need it (see the food storage tips on page 15).

Leftovers

Refrigerate for up to 3 days. Not suitable to freeze.

Anyone who knows me, knows about my love affair with cabbage. Cabbage is added to my grocery shop weekly, ready to bake, shred or stir-fry (check out my food storage tips on page 15). A single cabbage can go such a long way – make sure you check out the simple cabbage salad on page 38. Growing up, we ate it with everything and it wasn't unusual for meals to be served with cabbage prepared at least two ways. One of my favourite ways to eat cabbage is roasted and I can safely say that cabbage is the hero in this one-pan dish. As it roasts, it takes on all the flavour of the bacon and chicken, complete with sweet, caramelised edges. The golden broth is perfect with mashed potatoes or crispy bread … there are never any leftovers so make extra if you want to enjoy some the next day.

5–6 bone-in chicken thigh cutlets, skin on
80 ml (⅓ cup) olive oil
1 teaspoon sweet paprika
1 teaspoon sea salt flakes
½ teaspoon freshly ground black pepper
200 g streaky bacon, cut into wide strips
1 onion, finely sliced

½ savoy cabbage, coarsely shredded
1 teaspoon dijon mustard
3 tablespoons apple cider vinegar
2 tablespoons brown sugar
½ teaspoon chicken stock powder
1 tablespoon chopped flat-leaf parsley, to serve (optional)

Preheat the oven to 180°C fan-forced.

Marinate the chicken in the olive oil, paprika, salt and pepper.

Heat a large, heavy-based frying pan over medium heat and cook the chicken on both sides for 2–3 minutes until starting to turn golden brown. Set aside.

Add the bacon to the same pan and cook, stirring, for 2–3 minutes. Spoon out any excess fat if desired (leave 1 tablespoon for extra flavour). Add the onion and cook for 2–3 minutes until softened, then add the cabbage, dijon mustard, apple cider vinegar, brown sugar, chicken stock powder and 125 ml (½ cup) water. Cook, covered, for 6–8 minutes until the cabbage has softened.

Return the chicken to the pan, skin-side up, and bake, uncovered, for 40 minutes or until the chicken is golden and cooked through. Leave to rest for 10 minutes, then sprinkle with the parsley (if using) and serve.

Caramelised spiced pumpkin

PREP TIME: 5 minutes

COOK TIME: 1 hour 30 minutes

SERVES: 4

Leftovers

Refrigerate the freshly cooked pumpkin leftovers for up to 3 days. Not suitable to freeze.

Make ahead

Roast the butternut pumpkin as per the recipe and refrigerate it for up to 3 days prior to eating. Reheat in a 180°C fan-forced oven for 15 minutes or until warmed through.

Cook once, eat twice

Use leftovers mashed into arancini (page 174) or add to salads.

This dish makes it seem as though you have spent hours in the kitchen, yet it only takes you minutes to prepare and uses just a handful of ingredients. I make this for most special occasions, particularly if I'm feeding a crowd. The oven does all the hard work and you're left with a vegetarian dish that can hold up on its own (served with salad and canned lentils dressed in lemon juice and olive oil) or as an amazing side to a roast or barbecued meat. There is beauty in being able to scoop the soft, sweet, caramelised pumpkin directly from the skin and the leftovers never go unused – they are delicious in salads and perfect for quick lunches.

1 butternut pumpkin, halved
  lengthways, seeds removed
1½ teaspoons sea salt flakes
1 teaspoon ground cumin
1 teaspoon sweet paprika
1 teaspoon brown sugar
½ teaspoon freshly ground
  black pepper

3 tablespoons olive oil
150 g crumbled Persian feta
1 handful coriander or flat-leaf
  parsley leaves
1 tablespoon pomegranate seeds
  (optional)

Preheat the oven to 180°C fan-forced.

Prepare the pumpkin by scoring a diamond-shaped pattern into the cut side. Remove the seeds and pulp.

Arrange the pumpkin on a deep baking tray and sprinkle it with the salt, cumin, paprika, brown sugar and pepper. Drizzle with the olive oil and use your hands to coat the cut side of the pumpkin. Roast for 1½ hours, adding 125 ml (½ cup) water to the baking dish halfway through cooking.

Sprinkle the pumpkin with the feta and coriander or parsley, and pomegranate seeds (if using). Serve whole, family-style, with a spoon for everyone to scoop directly from the pumpkin.

Comforting country chicken pie

PREP TIME: 10 minutes

COOK TIME: 55 minutes

SERVES: 4

Hot tip

Whenever I find free-range chicken thigh fillets on special, I buy extra and make a double batch of this pie filling to freeze.

Leftovers

Refrigerate freshly made pie leftovers for up to 3 days. Freeze for up to 2 months. Thaw completely in the fridge overnight before reheating. The puff pastry will soften during the reheating process (even in the oven) but the pie filling is equally delicious.

Make ahead

You can make the pie filling up to 3 days in advance. Refrigerate, then top with the pastry and bake as per the recipe. Alternatively, freeze the assembled pie, covered in foil, for up to 2 months. Remove from the freezer for 30 minutes before baking (do not thaw). First bake, covered in foil, for 30 minutes, then bake as per the recipe.

This pie is the ultimate comfort food that requires no special equipment. It's on repeat at my place because how could you not want to eat flaky golden pastry filled with chicken and country veg smothered in a delicious creamy gravy regularly? I use store-bought puff pastry as I'm all about the 'working smarter not harder' life. You'll be blown away by the flavour you are able to create with minimal effort. It's easily adaptable for you to use any vegetables you like based on what's in season, but I love the classic carrot, peas and potato trifecta. It's the best!

1 tablespoon olive oil
1 onion, finely diced
1 celery stalk, roughly diced
1 large carrot, peeled and roughly diced
500 g chicken thigh fillets, cut into bite-sized pieces
1½ teaspoons sea salt flakes
½ teaspoon freshly ground black pepper
2 potatoes, peeled and cut into small cubes (no larger than 1 cm)
40 g unsalted butter

50 g (⅓ cup) plain flour
375 ml (1½ cups) chicken stock
250 ml (1 cup) full-cream milk
1 teaspoon dijon mustard
1 teaspoon dried thyme
80 g (½ cup) frozen peas
100 g (1 cup) freshly grated parmesan
1½ sheets frozen puff pastry, partially thawed, cut into rectangles roughly 6 cm x 3 cm
1 egg, whisked
1 teaspoon sesame seeds

Heat the olive oil in a large frying pan over medium–high heat. Add the onion, celery and carrot and cook, stirring, for 4–5 minutes until softened. Add the chicken, 1 teaspoon salt and the pepper and cook, stirring, for a further 3–5 minutes until browned.

Add the potato and butter to the pan and stir them in. Once the butter has melted, add the flour and stir to form a thick paste. Stirring constantly, slowly pour in the chicken stock followed by the milk. Add the dijon mustard and dried thyme and stir them through. Bring the mixture to the boil, then reduce the heat to the lowest setting and simmer, uncovered, for 10 minutes or until the potatoes are tender.

Remove the pan from the heat. Add the peas and parmesan and stir them through, then allow the mixture to cool.

Preheat the oven to 200°C fan-forced.

Spoon the cooled mixture into a pie dish. Layer the top with the thawed puff pastry rectangles so they slightly overlap each other. Brush with the egg, season with the remaining salt and sprinkle with the sesame seeds. Bake for 30–35 minutes or until the pastry is golden and crispy.

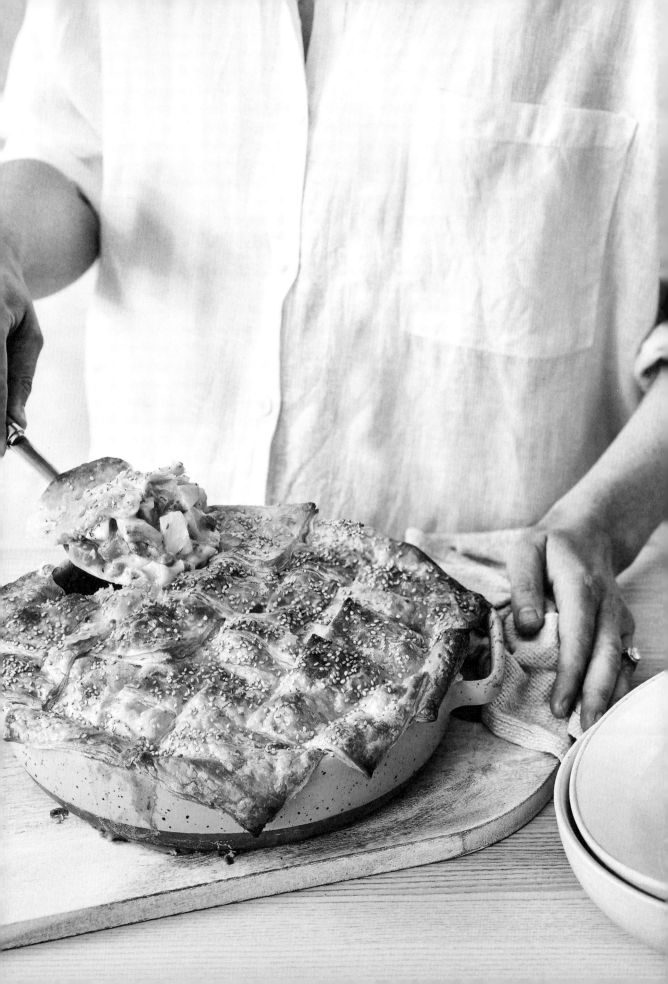

'Hidden veg' meatballs in rich tomato sauce

PREP TIME: 15 minutes

COOK TIME: 30 minutes

SERVES: 4

Note

Change up the veg! Use 2 cups of any veg you like, cutting or grating them finely so they melt into the sauce. Don't omit the onion, garlic or carrot as these create depth of flavour.

Leftovers

Refrigerate leftovers for up to 3 days. Freeze for up to 3 months. Thaw completely in the fridge overnight before reheating.

Make ahead

Meatballs Freeze uncooked meatballs for up to 2 months. Freeze on a flat tray, then transfer to an airtight container. Bake from frozen, but add 10 minutes to the cook time.

Sauce Freeze the sauce separately for up to 3 months in an airtight container. Thaw completely in the fridge before reheating.

Cook once, eat twice

Make meatballs sub sandwiches with leftovers. Fill crunchy baguettes with left-over meatballs and extra cheese before grilling them. Top with shredded lettuce, pickles and burger sauce (page 172).

My family loves meatballs, but searing them and watching them splatter all over the stovetop is my idea of torture. I am all about minimal effort when it comes to weeknight dinners, so you can imagine my satisfaction, dropping these raw meatballs directly into a veggie-loaded sauce, then popping them in the oven to cook to perfection. There is not a dry meatball in sight (in fact, these are the best meatballs I've ever eaten) AND my stovetop remains intact. The sauce is made with a heap of vegetables and you're not limited to those listed. Those broccoli stalks, cauliflower florets or spinach leaves that need to be used up in the crisper? They can all be grated, shredded or finely chopped and added to this dish. I love the extra boost my kids get from the veggies in this sauce – particularly the ones they would normally turn their noses up at eating!

MEATBALLS
- 500 g beef mince
- ½ onion, finely grated
- 65 g (⅔ cup) dried breadcrumbs
- 1 teaspoon sea salt flakes
- ½ teaspoon freshly ground black pepper
- 1 egg
- 1 tablespoon full-cream milk
- 1 tablespoon freshly grated parmesan
- 1 tablespoon finely chopped flat-leaf parsley

SAUCE
- 2 tablespoons olive oil
- 1 onion, finely grated
- 1 teaspoon finely chopped garlic
- 1 zucchini, finely grated
- 1 carrot, peeled and finely grated
- 1 celery stalk, finely diced
- 200 g mushrooms, finely diced
- 2 tablespoons tomato paste
- 700 g jar passata
- 500 ml (2 cups) beef stock
- 1 teaspoon sea salt flakes
- 1 teaspoon sugar
- ½ teaspoon freshly ground black pepper
- 150 g (1 cup) freshly grated mozzarella
- basil leaves, to serve
- crusty bread, to serve

Preheat the oven to 200°C fan-forced.

For the meatballs, combine all the ingredients in a large bowl. Use an ice-cream scoop to help measure out roughly 1 tablespoon portions of the mixture and roll into balls. Set aside.

For the sauce, heat the olive oil in a large, deep flame-proof baking dish over medium–high heat. Add the onion, garlic, zucchini, carrot, celery and mushrooms and cook, stirring, for 4–5 minutes until softened.

Add the tomato paste to the dish and stir it through, then add the passata, beef stock, salt, sugar and pepper. Bring the sauce to a simmer.

Drop the meatballs into the sauce and spoon the sauce over them so they are covered (it's fine if they are not completely submerged).

Sprinkle the meatballs with the mozzarella and bake for 18–20 minutes until the cheese is golden and the meatballs are cooked through. Sprinkle with the basil and serve with some crusty bread.

One-pan peanut chicken

PREP TIME: 8 minutes

COOK TIME: 50 minutes

SERVES: 4

Leftovers

Refrigerate for up to 2 days. Not suitable to freeze.

Make ahead

Prepare the steamed greens in advance using the food storage tips on page 15.

A couple of months ago I had some coconut milk in the freezer that I needed to use up, and a hankering for chicken satay. I made this amazing one-pan peanut chicken and we haven't been able to stop eating it since. Chicken thigh cutlets are an amazing, quick dinner fix at the best of times, as they're inexpensive and relatively hands-off to prepare. In this recipe, the luxurious peanut and coconut sauce is poured directly onto the chicken, which is roasted until juicy and crispy skinned. It's outrageously delicious and I'm left with only one pan to wash up. The sauce is rich and there's a lot of it (high sauce to chicken ratios are non negotiable at my place!), so a big plate of steamed greens is the perfect accompaniment. I've gone with bok choy; choose whatever's in season.

1.2 kg bone-in, skin-on chicken
   thigh cutlets, (5–6 pieces)
1½ teaspoons sea salt flakes
1 teaspoon sweet paprika
1 teaspoon onion powder
½ teaspoon freshly ground
   black pepper
3 tablespoons olive oil

SAUCE
1 teaspoon freshly grated garlic
1 teaspoon freshly grated ginger
250 ml (1 cup) coconut milk
90 g (⅓ cup) natural smooth
   peanut butter

½ teaspoon dark soy sauce
2 tablespoons tamari or soy sauce
2 tablespoons runny honey
1 tablespoon freshly squeezed lime
   juice (or rice wine vinegar)

TO SERVE
crushed peanuts
coriander leaves
sliced bird's eye chilli (optional)
steamed bok choy
steamed jasmine rice
lime wedges

Preheat the oven to 180°C fan-forced.

Pat the chicken dry using paper towel. Place it in a large bowl and sprinkle it with the salt, paprika, onion powder and pepper. Drizzle with the olive oil and use your hands to ensure the chicken is evenly coated.

Arrange the chicken on a large deep baking tray and bake for 35 minutes. Spoon out/drain away any excess fat in the tray.

For the sauce, combine the ingredients in a bowl, then pour the mixture into the pan around the chicken. Bake for a further 15 minutes.

Top with the peanuts, coriander and sliced chilli (if using). Serve with the steamed bok choy and jasmine rice with the lime wedges on the side.

Roasted Mediterranean vegetable salad

PREP TIME: 20 minutes

COOK TIME: 35 minutes

SERVES: 4

Note

Optional add-ons: Roasted pine nuts, rocket or baby spinach leaves, cooked quinoa, couscous or risoni, pesto, feta or goat's cheese.

Leftovers

Once dressed and combined with fresh herbs, the salad is best consumed within 24 hours (the herbs will darken).

Make ahead

Vegetables Refrigerate for up to 3 days. Do not dress. Bring to room temperature for 30 minutes before dressing and adding the herbs.

Dressing Refrigerate separately for up to 3 days.

Cook once, eat twice

Toss the roasted veg through pasta with 2–3 tablespoons pesto and a dusting of parmesan for a quick and easy Mediterranean pesto pasta.

There are certain vegetables that belong together and for me those are eggplant, zucchini and capsicum. Together they create the most amazing flavour, especially when roasted until caramelised on the outside and tender on the inside. The beauty of this salad is that it can be prepared in advance, ready for when you need it, and it can be served warm or cold. It stands up on its own as a side dish for almost anything, or can be bulked out with quinoa, couscous or risoni. The veg really don't need a lot. I love them tossed with fresh herbs, canned chickpeas and lots of olive oil, but there are tons of add-ons you can try based on what is on special and what you need to use up in your fridge.

1 large eggplant, sliced (just under 1 cm thick)
2 zucchini, finely sliced (just under 1 cm thick)
1 red capsicum, cut into thick strips
1 red onion, cut into wedges
olive oil spray or 3 tablespoons olive oil, for brushing
1 teaspoon sea salt flakes
½ teaspoon freshly ground black pepper

BALSAMIC DRESSING
80 ml (⅓ cup) olive oil
2 tablespoons balsamic vinegar
1 teaspoon runny honey
1 teaspoon sea salt flakes
½ teaspoon freshly ground black pepper

SALAD
400 g can chickpeas, rinsed and drained
½ bunch flat-leaf parsley, leaves picked
½ bunch mint, leaves picked

Preheat the oven to 220°C fan-forced.

Arrange the vegetables on a baking tray lined with baking paper – use two trays if required so the vegetables are not overlapping. Spray or brush the vegetables generously with olive oil, then sprinkle with the salt and pepper. Roast for 35 minutes or until caramelised and golden, swapping and rotating the trays halfway through cooking. At the halfway mark, flip the eggplant (the remaining vegetables do not need to be flipped over) and remove the onion and set aside (it takes a lot less time to cook).

For the dressing, combine all the ingredients in a jug and whisk well.

To assemble the salad, toss the vegetables, chickpeas, parsley and mint with the dressing and serve.

Golden beef pot pies

PREP TIME: 10 minutes

COOK TIME: 55 minutes

SERVES: 4

Leftovers

If made fresh, leftovers can be stored in the fridge for up to 3 days. Reheat in the microwave (although the puff pastry will soften, the pie will be equally delicious!) or in the oven to retain the puff pastry crunch.

Make ahead

Prepare the beef filling as per the recipe, then refrigerate for up to 48 hours or freeze for up to 2 months. Thaw overnight in the fridge. The filling does not need to be reheated before baking.

These beef pot pies are a 'core meal' (see page 11 to learn more) that I lean into regularly on our meal plan. My kids love beef pies, so naturally this homemade version is popular at our place. I serve whole veggies on the side with most meals, but I also love to pack vegetables into sauces and stews wherever possible. This recipe includes carrot and celery, but you can also finely grate and add whatever veg you have in the fridge (like zucchini or left-over broccoli stalks) and they melt into the most delicious, flavour-packed gravy. This recipe uses beef mince so it doesn't break the bank and it's a comforting, cosy meal that comes together quickly and with minimal effort.

1 tablespoon olive oil
1 large onion, finely diced
2 garlic cloves, finely chopped
2 carrots, peeled and grated
2 celery stalks, finely diced
750 g beef mince
2 tablespoons tomato paste
2 tablespoons plain flour
2 tablespoons Worcestershire sauce

500 ml (2 cups) beef stock
½ teaspoon freshly ground
  black pepper
1–2 sheets frozen puff pastry,
  partially thawed
1 egg, whisked
1 teaspoon sea salt flakes
steamed peas, to serve
ketchup, to serve

Heat the olive oil in a large, heavy-based saucepan over high heat. Add the onion, garlic, carrot and celery and cook, stirring, for 4–5 minutes until softened. Add the beef mince and cook for 4–5 minutes until browned, breaking it up as you go.

Add the tomato paste to the pan and stir to combine. Sprinkle in the flour and stir to combine. Add the Worcestershire sauce, beef stock and pepper. Bring to a gentle simmer, cover and cook on the lowest setting for 20–25 minutes, stirring occasionally. If the mixture starts to stick to the bottom of the pan, add 3 tablespoons water and stir through.

Preheat the oven to 200°C fan-forced.

Cut the pastry into four squares. Divide the beef mixture between four oven-proof ramekins (roughly 300 ml capacity each).

Lay a square of pastry on top of each ramekin and, using your fingers, pinch and tuck the pastry around the edge of the dish to seal. Brush the egg over the top of each pie and sprinkle on the salt.

Bake for 20 minutes or until the pastry is golden and crisp. Serve with the steamed peas and ketchup.

Baked chicken parmigiana

PREP TIME: 20 minutes

COOK TIME: 25 minutes

SERVES: 4

Leftovers

Refrigerate cooked chicken schnitzel for up to 3 days. The crumbing will soften but will be equally delicious. Freeze left-over pasta sauce for up to 2 months in a reusable sandwich bag or airtight container. Left-over grated or sliced mozzarella can be frozen for up to 4 weeks.

Make ahead

Once the chicken is crumbed, you can refrigerate it, uncooked, in an airtight container, for up to 3 days. Or freeze it in a large airtight container for up to 6 weeks – layer the chicken between pieces of baking paper to stop the chicken sticking together. Thaw completely in the fridge overnight and cook as per the recipe.

Cook once, eat twice

Enjoy the baked chicken schnitzels with Creamy Potato Salad (page 120) or try mashed potato and creamy mushroom sauce (page 29). Leftovers also make great chicken schnitzel sandwiches in lunch boxes or work well on top of caesar salad (page 126).

Tell me that eating a pub-style classic in pyjamas and slippers isn't the ultimate night in! This is the perfect meal to make on the days where you have a little bit of extra time up your sleeve. Crumbing schnitzels may seem like a lot of effort, but it's surprisingly simple and this meal comes with the added bonus of being able to be made in bulk and frozen. I often brave scattered breadcrumbs across the kitchen floor and get the kids involved to help. The baking paper tip makes cleaning up a breeze. A few extra tips ensure that the chicken is juicy and tender every time (no dry chicken in sight) and perfectly golden.

120 g (2 cups) panko breadcrumbs
olive oil spray
2 large chicken breast fillets,
    cut in half horizontally to make
    4 steaks
1 teaspoon sea salt flakes
½ teaspoon freshly ground
    black pepper
150 g (1 cup) plain flour

2 eggs, whisked
250 g (1 cup) tomato pasta sauce
75 g (½ cup) sliced or shredded
    mozzarella
2 tablespoons freshly grated
    parmesan, plus extra to serve
¼ bunch basil, leaves picked,
    to serve

Preheat the oven to 200°C fan-forced.

Arrange the breadcrumbs on a baking tray lined with baking paper and spray with the olive oil. Bake for 5–8 minutes or until golden, stirring halfway through cooking. Set aside while you prepare the remaining ingredients.

Lay a piece of baking paper on top of the chicken, then use a mallet or rolling pin to pound it to an even thickness.

Sprinkle the chicken with salt and pepper, using your hands to ensure the chicken is evenly coated. (The salt is what keeps the chicken moist and stops it drying out in the oven, so don't skip this step.)

To set up your crumbing station, spread the flour out on a large piece of baking paper, spread the toasted breadcrumbs out on a separate large piece of baking paper, then have the whisked egg ready in a large shallow bowl.

Press both sides of a chicken piece into the flour, then into the egg (allowing any excess to drip off), and lastly press the chicken into the breadcrumbs, ensuring all sides are evenly coated. Transfer to a plate.

Use the baking paper to help shuffle the flour and breadcrumbs into the centre of the baking paper, ready for the next piece of chicken. Repeat the crumbing process with the remaining pieces of chicken.

Place the chicken on a wire rack sitting on a baking tray – this produces the best results, helping the chicken stay crispy all over, but if you don't have one, you can use a regular baking tray.

Spray the schnitzels with olive oil and cook for 12–15 minutes or until the chicken is cooked through and the juices run clear.

Preheat the oven grill to high.

Arrange the chicken on a baking tray lined with baking paper and top each piece of chicken with the tomato pasta sauce, mozzarella and parmesan. Spray with olive oil and grill the chicken for 2 minutes or until the cheese is golden and bubbling.

Top with the basil leaves and serve with a simple green salad and Crunchy Seasoned Potato Wedges (page 190).

Pasta. Fresh ideas using the ultimate pantry staple

Summer pasta with garlic sourdough crumb

PREP TIME: 10 minutes

COOK TIME: 20 minutes

SERVES: 4

Hot tip

Feeling fancy? Serve the spaghetti on a platter topped with torn burrata.

Leftovers

Refrigerate for up to 3 days. Not suitable to freeze.

Make ahead

Breadcrumbs Prepare as per the recipe (but do not add the parmesan). Store in an airtight container for up to 5 days.

On the afternoon I made this dish for the first time, I called my daughter over for a taste test. Our 'taste test' ended up being a 3 pm dinner with us not being able to twirl the spaghetti onto our forks fast enough! This pasta is so unassumingly delicious, simple and speedy. The tomatoes are popped onto a baking tray with garlic and olive oil and roasted until tender, before being tossed with spaghetti and fresh basil. The whole thing is then topped with generous amounts of garlicky sourdough breadcrumbs. Do you need them? You do. They are just so delicious and well worth the extra effort. Make them ahead of time because no one, myself included, wants to whip out their food processor on a weeknight. You'll find yourself sprinkling them on everything – salads and steamed veggies LOVE them.

600 g cherry tomatoes
½ red onion, finely chopped
1 tablespoon finely chopped garlic
1 teaspoon dried oregano
1 teaspoon sugar
1 teaspoon sea salt flakes
3 tablespoons olive oil
400 g spaghetti
½ bunch basil, leaves picked

GARLIC SOURDOUGH CRUMB
4 slices sourdough bread
1 tablespoon olive oil
20 g butter
½ teaspoon freshly grated garlic
1 teaspoon sea salt flakes
35 g (⅓ cup) freshly grated parmesan

Preheat the oven to 200°C fan-forced.

For the sourdough crumb, blend the sourdough in a food processor to a coarse crumb. Heat the olive oil in a frying pan over medium heat and add the butter. Once melted, immediately add the breadcrumbs and cook, stirring, for 3–4 minutes or until golden. Add the garlic and salt and stir for 30 seconds. Remove from the heat. Once the sourdough crumb is cool, add the parmesan and stir it through. Set aside.

Place the cherry tomatoes, red onion, garlic, oregano, sugar, salt and olive oil in a baking dish. Toss to combine, then bake for 15–20 minutes until the tomatoes are softened.

Meanwhile, cook the spaghetti as per the packet instructions. Reserve 125 ml (½ cup) pasta cooking water (take it out of the pan with a ladle or mug while the pasta is cooking).

Drain, then toss the spaghetti with the tomatoes, reserved pasta cooking water and basil leaves. Sprinkle the sourdough crumb over the pasta and serve.

Chicken boscaiola pasta

Hot tip

Need an extra hit of veggies? Add a few handfuls of grated zucchini, baby spinach leaves or frozen peas at the same time as the mushrooms.

Leftovers

Refrigerate for up to 2 days. Not suitable to freeze.

I was quite a picky eater growing up, even through my teen years. It was only when I started waitressing in restaurants that my interest and curiosity in food developed. 'Boscaiola' sauce used to be all the rage back then – a creamy bacon and mushroom sauce tossed through pasta. More than 20 years later, it is still so popular and I promise you that once you make this incredible homemade version with the addition of chicken, you'll never want to order this at a restaurant again. This dish is everything. Not only is it quick and easy to make, with fresh, simple ingredients, it is rich and flavour packed – perfect comfort food to enjoy at the end of a long day. Try it with the freezer-friendly garlic bread on page 86.

2 large chicken breast fillets, cut in half horizontally to make 4 steaks
1 teaspoon sweet paprika
1 teaspoon sea salt flakes
1 teaspoon freshly ground black pepper
1 tablespoon olive oil
200 g streaky bacon, cut into wide strips
20 g unsalted butter
1 small onion, finely diced
1 tablespoon finely chopped garlic
400 g fettuccine
200 g Swiss brown mushrooms, sliced
300 ml thickened cream
½ teaspoon chicken stock powder
100 g (1 cup) freshly grated parmesan, plus extra to serve
1 tablespoon finely chopped flat-leaf parsley, to serve

Sprinkle the chicken with the paprika, salt and half the pepper.

Heat the olive oil in a large, heavy-based frying pan over medium–high heat and cook the chicken for 6–8 minutes until golden and just cooked, turning once halfway through cooking. Slice the chicken into thin strips and set aside.

Add the bacon to the same pan and cook for 2 minutes or until crisp. Use a spoon to scoop out any excess bacon fat if required. Add the butter and, once melted, add the onion and garlic. Cook, stirring, for 2 minutes until softened.

Meanwhile, cook the fettuccine as per the packet instructions minus 1 minute. Reserve 125 ml (½ cup) cooking water (take it out of the pot using a ladle or mug while the pasta is cooking). Drain.

Add the mushrooms to the bacon mixture and cook, stirring, for 3–4 minutes until softened. Add the thickened cream, reserved pasta cooking water, chicken stock powder and remaining pepper and simmer for 2 minutes until thickened.

Remove the pan from the heat, add the parmesan, pasta and chicken and stir them through. Serve with the extra parmesan and sprinkled with parsley.

Creamy rose pasta with pork sausage

PREP TIME: 5 minutes

COOK TIME: 12 minutes

SERVES: 4

Leftovers

Refrigerate for up to 2 days. Freeze for up to 2 months. Thaw completely in the fridge overnight before reheating.

Any dish that creates an incredible depth of flavour with very few simple ingredients and little prep is what I call a triumph. Whenever I meal plan, I consider dishes that will suit the time constraints. This is what I make when I need something super speedy and next-level delicious. Standard supermarket sausages are given a glow-up, cooked until golden and crisp before being adorned with a creamy, garlicky, tomato and parmesan–filled sauce, all finished with a few handfuls of spinach. Dinner is on the table in less than 20 minutes and there's very little washing up. This dish is versatile and gives you the flexibility to add whatever vegetables you like – try zucchini, broccoli, green beans, frozen peas, capsicum or mushrooms. Add them immediately after browning the sausages and cook them for a few minutes for an extra hit of veg.

400 g rigatoni
1 tablespoon olive oil
500 g pork and fennel sausages, meat squeezed from casings
1 tablespoon freshly grated garlic
1 tablespoon tomato paste
400 g can crushed tomatoes
250 ml (1 cup) thickened cream

90 g (2 cups) baby spinach leaves
½ teaspoon sea salt flakes
½ teaspoon freshly ground black pepper
100 g (1 cup) freshly grated parmesan, plus extra to serve
¼ bunch basil, leaves picked, to serve

Cook the rigatoni as per the packet directions minus 1 minute. Reserve 125 ml (½ cup) pasta cooking water (take it out of the pot using a ladle or mug while the pasta is cooking). Drain.

Meanwhile, heat the olive oil in a large, heavy-based frying pan over medium–high heat, add the sausages and cook, turning, for 3–4 minutes until golden, breaking them up as you go. Add the garlic and cook for 30 seconds.

Add the tomato paste and stir it through for 30 seconds, then add the crushed tomatoes, thickened cream, baby spinach, salt and pepper. Simmer for about 5–6 minutes until the sauce begins to thicken. Add the parmesan and the cooked pasta and stir them through – add the reserved pasta cooking water to loosen the sauce if needed. Serve with the extra parmesan and basil leaves.

Spinach & ricotta lasagne parcels

PREP TIME: 15 minutes

COOK TIME: 30 minutes

SERVES: 4–6

Note

This recipe must be made with fresh lasagne sheets, which are pliable and can be folded to enclose the ricotta filling. They can be found in the refrigerated section of the supermarket.

Leftovers

Refrigerate for up to 3 days. Freeze cooked, individual portions for up to 2 months. Thaw completely in the fridge overnight before reheating.

Make ahead

Refrigerate the whole, uncooked lasagne for up to 3 days or freeze for up to 2 months. Bake from frozen, allow 1 hour and cover with foil for the first 30 minutes.

I love ALL versions of lasagne but not that much on those nights where I don't have the time or energy to be fussing, layering and dealing with the aftermath of a kitchen sink filled with multiple pots and pans. With this version, ricotta and spinach are enclosed in lasagne sheets to make little parcels, then topped with store-bought pasta sauce, pesto and cheese. This recipe is so easy to make yet the flavour payoff is amazing considering it's made with so little. It's perfect for the nights when you need something fast and nothing other than a delicious, homemade lasagne will do. My mouth is watering just thinking about it!

250 g fresh pasta sheets (see Note)
800 g tomato pasta sauce
60 g (¼ cup) basil pesto, store-bought or homemade
150 g (1 cup) freshly grated mozzarella
basil leaves, to serve

SPINACH AND RICOTTA FILLING
500 g frozen spinach, thawed and drained
500 g fresh ricotta
50 g (½ cup) freshly grated parmesan
1 teaspoon sea salt flakes
½ teaspoon freshly ground black pepper

To make the spinach and ricotta filling, in a bowl combine the thawed and drained frozen spinach with the ricotta, parmesan, salt and pepper.

Preheat the oven to 180°C fan-forced.

Place six lasagne sheets on your kitchen bench, then divide the ricotta and spinach mixture across one half of each of the sheets. Fold each sheet in half to create a parcel, so that the filling is enclosed, crossways.

Spoon 125 g (½ cup) pasta sauce into the bottom of a baking dish. Top with three lasagne parcels, side by side (it's okay if they are slightly overlapping). Spoon half of the remaining pasta sauce over them so the lasagne sheets are completely covered. Dollop tablespoons of the pesto over the top. Place the remaining three lasagne parcels on top. Top with the remaining pasta sauce and sprinkle with the mozzarella.

Bake the lasagne, uncovered, for 30 minutes or until golden and cooked through. Top with the basil leaves and rest for 5 minutes before serving.

Prawn pasta with freezer-friendly garlic bread

PREP TIME: 10 minutes

COOK TIME: 12 minutes

SERVES: 4

Leftovers

Prawn spaghetti is best cooked and served immediately. Leftovers can be refrigerated for up to 2 days and reheated in the microwave, taking care not to overheat and cause the prawns to turn rubbery.

Make ahead

You can freeze the garlic bread for up to 2 months in foil. To bake, remove from the freezer (leave wrapped in foil) and bake in a preheated 180°C fan-forced oven for 18–22 minutes.

This dish may be the weekend meal that you look forward to as a family, or a special date-night meal, or it may just be the dinner you need after any long day. For me, this prawn pasta with crispy, delicious garlic bread has been all of those things. This dish comes together so quickly – the longest part of the process is waiting for the pasta water to boil. Lots of garlic and little bursts of cherry tomatoes combine to make the most delicious sauce, and while the pasta is perfect on its own, my freezer is never without this incredible garlic bread, which is the ideal accompaniment to any pasta meal.

FREEZER-FRIENDLY GARLIC BREAD
- 1 ciabatta loaf
- 80 g unsalted butter, softened
- 2 teaspoons finely chopped garlic
- ½ teaspoon sea salt flakes
- 1 tablespoon finely chopped flat-leaf parsley
- 75 g (½ cup) freshly grated mozzarella (optional)

PRAWNS
- 16–20 raw prawns, peeled and deveined, tails intact
- ½ teaspoon sweet paprika
- ½ teaspoon sea salt flakes
- ½ teaspoon freshly ground black pepper

PASTA
- 400 g spaghetti
- 80 ml (⅓ cup) olive oil
- 1 tablespoon finely chopped garlic

- ½ red onion, finely diced
- 200 g cherry tomatoes
- 1 teaspoon sea salt flakes, plus extra to serve
- 1 teaspoon freshly ground black pepper
- 2 tablespoons tomato paste
- 100 g (1 cup) freshly grated parmesan, plus extra to serve
- 2 tablespoons finely chopped flat-leaf parsley

For the garlic bread, preheat the oven to 180°C fan-forced. Cut the bread into 1.5 cm slices, taking care not to cut all the way through to the base. Combine the butter, garlic, salt and parsley. Spread the butter mixture over each side of the sliced bread. Stuff each slice with a big pinch of mozzarella (if using). Wrap the loaf in foil (see Make Ahead for freezing instructions). If serving immediately, bake the foil-wrapped garlic bread for 15–18 minutes until golden and crisp.

For the prawns, combine the prawns, paprika, salt and pepper in a small bowl. Toss to coat. Do not marinate for longer than 20 minutes.

For the pasta, cook the spaghetti as per the packet instructions minus 1 minute. Reserve 250 ml (1 cup) pasta cooking water (take it out of the pot using a ladle or mug while the pasta is cooking). Drain.

Meanwhile, heat 2 tablespoons olive oil in a large frying pan over medium–high heat. Add the prawns and cook for 1 minute on each side. Remove the prawns from the pan and set aside.

Add the remaining 2 tablespoons olive oil, the garlic and red onion to the same pan and stir for 30 seconds until fragrant. Add 125 ml (½ cup) pasta cooking water.

Add the cherry tomatoes, salt and pepper and cook for 2–3 minutes. Squash the tomatoes with the back of a fork to release their juices. Add the tomato paste and the remaining pasta cooking water and stir through. Add the spaghetti and parmesan and stir through. Add the prawns and parsley and stir them through, then serve immediately. Sprinkle with the extra parmesan and salt if desired.

One-pan pesto chicken pasta

PREP TIME: 10 minutes

COOK TIME: 15 minutes

SERVES: 4

Note

It's okay if some of the vegetables become submerged, but try not to stir them through, as they will steam as the pasta and sauce cook. It's important that the pasta remains submerged beneath the sauce as much as possible to ensure it cooks evenly.

Leftovers

Refrigerate for up to 3 days. Freeze for up to 2 months. For best results, thaw completely in the fridge overnight before reheating in the microwave or on the stovetop.

Make ahead

Prep the chicken and vegetables up to 3 days in advance for an extra-easy dinner.

There are days where time just isn't my friend. You know the kind of days … the ones filled with appointments, after-school activities or work commitments, the days when it would be so easy to cruise through a drive-through and call it a day. While the convenience of takeaway is welcomed at our place sometimes, this is the dinner I make when I want to get a home-cooked meal on the table effortlessly and with as little time spent in the kitchen as possible. This dish is made in one pan. And when I say one pan, I mean it. Uncooked pasta is tossed in and the starches released help to thicken the luxuriously creamy pesto sauce. You can use any vegetables of choice with this one, but my personal favourite is broccoli. I use the stalk and all, finely chopped, so there is no waste.

2 tablespoons olive oil
500 g chicken breast fillets, diced
1 teaspoon sea salt flakes, plus extra to taste
½ teaspoon freshly ground black pepper, plus extra to taste
40 g unsalted butter
1 tablespoon finely chopped garlic
750 ml (3 cups) chicken stock
375 ml (1½ cups) thickened cream

250 g short pasta (one that takes 8–9 minutes to cook)
1 head of broccoli, cut into florets, stalk finely sliced (or 2 cups chopped vegetables of choice)
2 tablespoons pesto, store-bought or homemade
100 g (1 cup) freshly grated parmesan
basil leaves, to serve (optional)

Heat the olive oil in a large frying pan over medium–high heat. Add the chicken, salt and pepper and cook, stirring, for 3–5 minutes until the chicken is just cooked through. Remove the chicken from the pan and set aside on a plate.

Add the butter to the same pan and, once melted, add the garlic and cook, stirring, for 30 seconds. Add the chicken stock and cream and bring to a gentle simmer. Add the pasta and cook for 4 minutes, uncovered, stirring occasionally.

Scatter the broccoli (or vegetables of choice) on top of the pasta (see Note). Cover and cook for 4 minutes, shuffling the pasta gently using a wooden spoon as required to ensure the pasta doesn't stick to the base of the pan.

Return the chicken to the pan, then add the pesto and parmesan and stir them through. Season with some extra salt and pepper to taste, add the basil leaves (if using) and serve.

Creamy bolognese pasta bake

PREP TIME: 10 minutes

COOK TIME: 1 hour 10 minutes

SERVES: 4–6

Leftovers

Refrigerate for up to 3 days. Freeze for up to 3 months. Thaw completely in the fridge overnight before reheating.

Bolognese is one of my favourite recipes and is a 'core meal' (see page 11) that we prepare at least fortnightly. There is something so wholesome about letting a big pot of bolognese sauce simmer on the stove for hours. This baked version is the perfect meal for when the craving hits but you're needing a fast (equally delicious) option. What could possibly make bolognese taste better than it already does? Thickened cream. Not only does it cut through the acidity of the tomatoes, it also adds an incredible depth of flavour and richness to the sauce. Combined with big spoonfuls of ricotta, you will want to eat this again and again. Try this dreamy dish with the freezer-friendly garlic bread on page 86.

2 tablespoons olive oil
1 red onion, finely diced
1 carrot, peeled and grated
1 celery stalk, finely diced
1 teaspoon finely chopped garlic
500 g beef mince
1 teaspoon sea salt flakes
½ teaspoon freshly ground
   black pepper
2 tablespoons tomato paste
2 x 400 g cans crushed tomatoes
250 ml (1 cup) beef stock

2 bay leaves
2 thyme sprigs (or 1 teaspoon
   dried thyme)
1 tablespoon sugar
125 ml (½ cup) thickened cream
400 g pasta spirals
200 g fresh ricotta
150 g (1 cup) freshly grated
   mozzarella
½ bunch basil, leaves picked,
   to serve (optional)

Heat the olive oil in a large oven-proof pot over medium–high heat. Add the onion, carrot, celery and garlic and cook, stirring, for 4–5 minutes until fragrant and softened.

Add the beef mince, salt and pepper and cook for 3–4 minutes until the meat is browned, breaking it up as you go. Add the tomato paste and stir it through for 30 seconds, then add the crushed tomatoes, beef stock, bay leaves, thyme, sugar and cream. Bring to a simmer, cover and cook for 45 minutes on the lowest heat setting.

Preheat the oven to 200°C fan-forced.

Cook the pasta as per the packet instructions minus 2 minutes. Drain, rinse in cold water and drain again.

Stir the cooked pasta through the creamy bolognese sauce. Top with tablespoons of ricotta and sprinkle with mozzarella. Transfer the mixture to a baking dish if required. Bake, uncovered, for 15 minutes or until golden and bubbly. Top with the basil leaves (if using) and serve.

Rice & noodles.

Bringing the flavour to your mid-week meals

Cheat's chicken laksa

PREP TIME: 5 minutes

COOK TIME: 8 minutes

SERVES: 4

Hot tip

Need an extra hit of vegetables? Add some frozen broccoli or green beans at the same time as the coconut milk and chicken stock. Need a mild spice? Add less red curry paste. Start with 1 tablespoon red curry paste and gradually add more.

Leftovers

This speedy laksa is best made fresh. Leftovers can be refrigerated for up to 2 days, although the liquid will absorb into the ingredients. Add 250 ml (1 cup) chicken stock to thin it out and create a soup consistency if required.

Thinking about laksa, I am immediately transported to my 20-something self, studying, finishing a late shift as a waitress and eating takeaway at 11 pm. My present self eats at around 4.30 pm. Oh how times have changed … Laksa is a dish I used to rule out for busy weeknights until I discovered this super-fast and easy version that takes less than 15 minutes to cook, prep time included! I love that there is very minimal chopping or fussing – everything just gets popped into the pan to simmer and in no time you have chicken and noodles in a comforting, rich, creamy coconut soup.

250 g ramen noodles, egg noodles or vermicelli rice noodles
2 tablespoons olive oil
500 g chicken thigh fillets, cut into bite-sized pieces
2 tablespoons Thai red curry paste
400 ml can coconut milk
2 litres chicken stock
200 g fried tofu puffs, cut in half using kitchen scissors
1 tablespoon fish sauce

2 tablespoons freshly squeezed lime juice
180 g (2 cups) bean sprouts

TO SERVE
fried shallots
spring onion, finely sliced
sliced bird's eye chilli (optional)
coriander leaves (optional)
lime wedges

Cook the noodles as per the packet instructions minus 1 minute. Drain, rinse in cold water, drain again and set aside.

In a large stockpot, heat the olive oil over high heat. Add the chicken and cook for 1–2 minutes until it begins to brown slightly. Stir in the curry paste and cook for 30 seconds. Add the coconut milk and chicken stock and cook for 2 minutes.

Add the fried tofu puffs, fish sauce and lime juice and cook for 2 minutes. Add half the bean sprouts and the cooked noodles. Turn the heat off.

Spoon into individual bowls and top with the remaining bean sprouts, the fried shallots, spring onion and the chilli and coriander (if using). Serve with lime wedges on the side.

Peanut butter pork & noodles

PREP TIME: 10 minutes

COOK TIME: 15 minutes

SERVES: 4

Leftovers

Refrigerate for up to 2 days.
Not suitable to freeze.

Creamy peanut butter tossed through noodles = genius. This recipe is made with simple pantry ingredients and is definitely something you need to try. When I meal plan I factor in tons of easy meals for when my energy levels are low and these peanut butter noodles are at the top of that list. The recipe uses inexpensive pork fillet, which is simple to prepare, cooks in a flash and is hard to get wrong – it is so tender and delicious. If pork isn't your thing, these noodles work equally well with chicken breast or chicken mince. I love using bean sprouts as the minimal chopping is always nice, but don't feel limited to these. ANY veg work in this satay-inspired dish – capsicum, mushrooms, broccoli, baby corn, carrots – if it's in season and in your crisper, it can absolutely be added to this recipe.

200 g egg noodles
1 tablespoon olive oil
400 g pork fillet, finely sliced
250 g bean sprouts, plus extra
  to serve
3 spring onions, cut into
  4 cm batons
crushed peanuts, to serve
chilli oil, to serve (optional)
lime wedges, to serve

PEANUT SAUCE
80 g (½ cup) natural smooth
  peanut butter
3 tablespoons tamari or soy sauce
2 tablespoons rice wine vinegar
1 tablespoon sugar
1 tablespoon sesame oil
1 teaspoon freshly grated garlic
1 teaspoon freshly grated ginger
125 ml (½ cup) chicken stock

Combine the peanut sauce ingredients in a bowl and set aside.

Prepare the egg noodles as per the packet instructions. Drain, rinse in cold water, drain again and set aside.

Heat the olive oil in a large, heavy-based frying pan over high heat. Add the pork and cook for 2–3 minutes until just cooked through. Add the bean sprouts, spring onion and peanut sauce and cook for 1 minute. Add 1–2 tablespoons water to thin the sauce if required.

Toss the noodles through the peanut sauce, then serve topped with extra bean sprouts, the crushed peanuts and chilli oil (if using). Serve with a squeeze of lime juice.

Classic fried rice

Note 1

How to cool freshly made rice Spread the cooked rice on a baking tray and place it in the fridge to cool for 30 minutes.

Note 2

How to freeze left-over rice Spread the cooked rice on a baking tray and allow it to cool for up to 15 minutes. Scoop it into freezer-safe containers (500 g portions, enough to serve 4) or microwave- and freezer–safe reusable sandwich bags. Freeze for up to 2 months. Thaw completely in the fridge overnight before using. Add to the fried rice cold, otherwise reheat in the microwave on High for 2–3 minutes until piping hot, ready for use.

Leftovers

If freshly cooked rice is used, fried rice can be refrigerated for up to 2 days or frozen for up to 2 months. Thaw in the fridge completely overnight before use. Reheat in the microwave. If left-over cooked rice is used, it is not recommended to store and reheat again.

One of my secret weapons to save time and money is to make extra plain rice and freeze it. If you open my freezer, you will find a stack of reusable sandwich bags filled with portions of rice. Cooked rice freezes beautifully and is so quick and easy to thaw in the microwave, ready to serve with your favourite dishes or to make this classic fried rice. When it comes to fried rice, less is more. Follow this recipe and be amazed by how little you need to make what is possibly the easiest takeaway dish to recreate at home. Once you are familiar with this basic recipe, you can add prawns or chicken (left-over roast chicken from the recipe on page 54 is perfect!) to bulk it out or replace the bacon with canned tuna for an extra-fast meal, but I love the fried rice on its own, especially with some chilli oil drizzled over.

1 tablespoon olive oil
200 g streaky bacon, diced
1 teaspoon finely chopped garlic
80 g (½ cup) frozen peas
75 g (½ cup) frozen corn kernels
4 eggs, whisked (1 egg per person)
555 g (3 cups) cold cooked rice, day-old or freshly made (see Notes)

2 spring onions, finely sliced
2 tablespoons sesame oil
2 tablespoons tamari or soy sauce
1 tablespoon fried shallots, to serve (optional)
chilli oil (optional)

Heat the olive oil in a large frying pan over medium–high heat. Add the bacon and cook for 2–3 minutes until golden. Add the garlic and cook, stirring, for 30 seconds.

Add the peas and corn to the pan. Cook for a further 1 minute, stirring, until the peas and corn are just thawed.

Push the ingredients to one side of the pan and add the egg. Cook for 2–3 minutes until the egg is firm, breaking it up as you go.

Add the rice, spring onion, sesame oil and tamari or soy sauce to the pan and stir gently to combine, or cook until the the rice is heated through. Serve topped with the fried shallots and drizzled with the chilli oil (if using).

Coconut red curry noodles

PREP TIME: 10 minutes

COOK TIME: 10 minutes

SERVES: 4

Leftovers

Refrigerate for up to 2 days. Not suitable to freeze.

Whenever I make these delicious creamy coconut noodles, I find myself hovering over the pan taking one too many bites to taste test. They are SO good. Their deliciousness, paired with how simple they are to make, has them frequenting our meal plan at least once a fortnight. The addition of tomato paste may seem strange, but it creates an amazing depth of flavour and mellows out the spice from the red curry paste – perfect for my little eaters who are still adapting to spicy foods. You can customise the vegetables to suit your family's tastes and swap out the mince for any other variety (both chicken mince or beef mince work really well). The noodles are customisable too – if egg noodles are all you have, throw those in, or just serve with rice. One thing I recommend is not skipping the lime at the end. That little pop of freshness is where it's at!

200 g thick rice noodles
1 tablespoon olive oil
500 g pork mince
1 tablespoon finely chopped garlic
1 teaspoon finely chopped ginger
2 tablespoons tomato paste
2 tablespoons red curry paste

400 ml can coconut milk
125 g green beans, trimmed, cut into 3–4 cm batons
1 red capsicum, cut into strips
crushed peanuts, to serve
1 lime, cut into wedges, to serve

Cook the rice noodles until just softened (this will take 2–3 minutes). Drain. Rinse immediately with cold tap water, then drain again – the noodles will still be undercooked and firm but will finish cooking in the pan.

Heat the olive oil in a large frying pan over medium–high heat. Add the pork mince and cook for 3–4 minutes until browned, breaking it up as you go. Add the garlic and ginger and cook, stirring, for 1 minute.

Add the tomato paste and red curry paste to the pan and stir them through. Add the coconut milk and green beans and cook for 2 minutes until the sauce has thickened.

Add the capsicum to the pan and cook for a further 1–2 minutes before stirring in the cooked noodles. Cook for a further 1–2 minutes or until just heated through.

Serve the noodles topped with the crushed peanuts and a squeeze of lime juice.

One-pot Greek chicken & rice

PREP TIME: 10 minutes

COOK TIME: 35 minutes

SERVES: 4

Note

You can substitute the vegetables to suit your family's tastes. Spinach, kale, silverbeet, sliced green beans, diced zucchini, peas or broccoli florets all work well.

Leftovers

Refrigerate for up to 3 days. Reheat in the microwave. Not suitable to freeze.

Make ahead

The chicken can be marinated up to 48 hours before cooking.

I'm not one to spend hours in the kitchen. As much as I enjoy leisurely cooking, most days I'm focused on getting dinner on the table before I'm too tired to cook or the kids are too tired to eat! I factor that in when I'm meal planning, and meals like this one swoop in and save the day every time. Chicken fillets are marinated in classic Greek flavours – think garlic, lemon and oregano – before being cooked in one pan with rice. The rice steals the show, being cooked in garlic and chicken stock while mingling with the chicken juices. Generous handfuls of spinach top it off so there is no need to fuss with any additional sides. This is my favourite kind of home cooking. Anyone who eats this stares at me bewildered at how delicious it is and I stare back at them knowingly, already getting ready to pass on the recipe.

600 g chicken thigh fillets, skin on (approximately 5–6 chicken thighs)
1 teaspoon finely chopped garlic
1 tablespoon dried oregano
½ teaspoon sweet paprika
½ teaspoon sea salt flakes
½ teaspoon freshly ground black pepper
zest of 1 lemon, plus 3 tablespoons freshly squeezed lemon juice
2 tablespoons olive oil

RICE
1 onion, finely diced
1 teaspoon finely chopped garlic
300 g (1½ cups) white rice (jasmine or basmati)
750 ml (3 cups) chicken stock
130 g (2 cups) roughly chopped spinach leaves (see Note)
½ teaspoon freshly ground black pepper

TO SERVE
1 tablespoon finely chopped flat-leaf parsley or oregano leaves
lemon slices and lemon zest (optional)
crumbled feta (optional)

Place the chicken thigh fillets in a large bowl with the garlic, dried oregano, paprika, salt, pepper, lemon zest, lemon juice and olive oil. Use your hands to coat the chicken evenly.

Heat a large, heavy-based oven-proof sauté pan over medium heat. Cook the chicken for 5–8 minutes until golden. Remove the chicken from the pan and set aside.

For the rice, add 1–2 tablespoons water to the same pan and stir to deglaze and loosen all the sticky bits, then add the onion and garlic. Cook, stirring for 2 minutes, until softened. Add the rice, chicken stock, spinach and pepper.

Return the chicken to the pan. Cover, reduce the heat to the lowest setting and cook for 20 minutes.

Remove the pan from the heat and let stand with the lid on for 10 minutes. This will allow for any residual liquid to be absorbed.

Top the chicken and rice with the parsley or oregano, lemon slices, lemon zest and feta (if using), then serve.

Quick chicken chow mein

PREP TIME: 20 minutes

COOK TIME: 5 minutes

SERVES: 4

Note

The time spent allowing the chicken to soften in the bicarbonate of soda is well worth the results, but if you are short on time, you can skip this step.

Leftovers

Refrigerate for up to 3 days. Reheat in the microwave. Not suitable to freeze.

Make ahead

Prepare the chicken and shred the vegetables up to 2 days before cooking for an extra fast, easy-to-put-together dinner.

If you've ever wondered how your favourite takeaway restaurants get the chicken so soft, this recipe will provide the answer. Chicken chow mein is another one of our 'core meals' (see page 11 to learn more). It's one of my favourite takeaway dishes and it also happens to be one of my favourites to replicate at home, made with simple ingredients. Marinating the chicken in bicarbonate of soda is what keeps the chicken incredibly soft and juicy. The sauce is light and flavourful and the dish can be packed with any veggies you like. Chicken chow mein is perfect for those nights where you don't want to make a big mess in the kitchen and need dinner on the table quickly … so, pretty much every night of the week at my place!

**500 g chicken breast fillet,
    finely sliced**
1 teaspoon bicarbonate of soda
250 g thin egg noodles
1 tablespoon cornflour
3 tablespoons tamari or soy sauce
1 teaspoon dark soy sauce
**1 tablespoon Shaoxing rice wine
    (Chinese cooking wine)**
1 tablespoon sesame oil

1 tablespoon sugar
2 garlic cloves, finely chopped
2 tablespoons olive oil
**150 g (2 cups) shredded green
    cabbage**
90 g (1 cup) julienned carrot
90 g (1 cup) bean sprouts
**3 spring onions, cut into
    3–4 cm batons**

Place the chicken in a bowl, sprinkle with the bicarbonate of soda and toss to coat evenly. Set aside for 20 minutes while you prepare the vegetables. This step is optional (see Note). Rinse the chicken well in a colander with tap water to remove the bicarbonate of soda, then dab it with paper towel to remove excess water.

Prepare the noodles as per the packet instructions. Drain and rinse in cold water to stop them from cooking, then drain again and set aside.

Prepare the sauce by mixing the cornflour and 3 tablespoons water together first. Then add the tamari or soy sauce, dark soy sauce, Shaoxing rice wine, sesame oil and sugar.

Drizzle 1 tablespoon of the sauce over the chicken and add the garlic. Toss so the chicken is evenly coated.

Heat the olive oil in a large frying pan over high heat and add the chicken. Cook for 1 minute until the chicken is sealed (it will still be raw in the centre).

Add the cabbage and carrot to the pan and cook, stirring, for 1–2 minutes until the cabbage softens. Add the noodles and sauce and cook for 1 minute. Add the bean sprouts and spring onion, stir them through, then cook for 30 seconds. Serve immediately.

Sticky Mongolian beef noodles

PREP TIME: 15 minutes

COOK TIME: 10 minutes

SERVES: 4

Note 1

A high smoke point oil (e.g. canola, vegetable or sunflower oil) is best for this recipe. It needs to be at least 2 cm deep in the pan.

Note 2

Cut the entire broccoli up, stalk and all! You can customise the vegetables in this recipe. Just use up to 3 cups of vegetables – try carrot, green beans, sugar snap peas, baby corn, capsicum, mushrooms or Asian greens.

Leftovers

Refrigerate for up to 3 days. Not suitable to freeze.

Make ahead

Prepare the vegetables in advance to make this an even speedier dinner. (See the food storage tips on page 15.)

Have you ever had takeaway and thought 'that wasn't worth it' or, 'I probably could have made that better'? While takeaway definitely has its place, there's nothing worse than ordering it and being disappointed, which is why I often end up making something myself. These sticky Mongolian beef noodles taste just like the real thing. The beef is super soft and tender thanks to cornflour (which tenderises any type of economical steak) and the sauce is thick, glossy, sticky and sweet. These noodles are made with simple ingredients and yet are just so outrageously delicious. The perfect way to end the week, this super-filling dish is customisable with whatever veg or noodles you like. Aside from being quick and easy, I love that I get four meals for the price I'd pay for just one if I ordered out. An amazing bonus!

350 g ramen noodles
400 g sirloin beef, finely sliced
1 teaspoon sea salt flakes
½ teaspoon freshly ground
    black pepper
30 g (¼ cup) cornflour
oil, for frying (see Note 1)
1 head of broccoli, cut into florets
    (see Note 2), or 2 bunches of
    broccolini, halved
1 onion, cut into thick slices
2 spring onions, cut into
    3–4 cm batons
125 ml (½ cup) water mixed with
    2 tablespoons cornflour
1 teaspoon sesame seeds, to serve

SAUCE
80 ml (⅓ cup) tamari or soy sauce
45 g (¼ cup) brown sugar
2 tablespoons sesame oil
1 tablespoon hoisin sauce
1 teaspoon freshly grated garlic
1 teaspoon freshly grated ginger

Cook the noodles as per the packet instructions, then drain and set aside.

Season the beef with the salt and pepper, then toss it in the cornflour.

Heat the oil in a large frying pan over high heat and cook the beef in batches for 2–3 minutes until browned. Reheat more oil in between batches if required. Remove the beef from the pan and set aside.

Wipe the pan clean using paper towel. Reduce the heat to medium–high and add the broccoli or broccolini and 125 (½ cup) water. Cover and steam the broccoli or broccolini for 2–3 minutes.

Meanwhile, combine the sauce ingredients in a small bowl, whisking well. Add the sauce to the pan and bring to a simmer. Immediately add the onion, spring onion, and water and cornflour mixture. Cook for 1–2 minutes, stirring until thickened and glossy. Return the beef to the pan and toss it through the sauce.

Divide the noodles among four bowls, top with the Mongolian beef, the broccoli or broccolini and a sprinkle of sesame seeds and serve.

Teriyaki chicken bowl

PREP TIME: 15 minutes

COOK TIME: 10 minutes

SERVES: 4

Note 1

Trim any excess fat and pound the chicken using a mallet or rolling pin to even out the thickness.

Note 2

You'll find edamame beans, already podded and ready to use, in the freezer section of your supermarket. Thaw as per the packet instructions.

Leftovers

Refrigerate cooked chicken for up to 2 days. Not suitable to freeze.

Make ahead

Make a batch of teriyaki marinade and refrigerate for up to 2 weeks, or marinate the chicken and refrigerate for up to 2 days. Freeze marinated chicken for up to 2 months. Thaw completely in the fridge overnight before cooking.

Cook once, eat twice

Try this marinade with beef mince and make beef teriyaki bowls.

I used to buy teriyaki marinade thinking that purchasing the individual ingredients to make my own would be too expensive … and then this amazing teriyaki chicken bowl entered my life. This is the best teriyaki marinade I've ever tried and it takes mere minutes to make. It's as easy as stirring together some pantry sauces (that can all be repurposed in other recipes). It's just amazing on nights where even the thought of peeling a garlic clove is too much. I love to serve this sweet and savoury chicken on rice with a big dollop of whole-egg mayonnaise and salads of choice. I told my kids that I got the recipe from our local sushi place and they immediately declared their love for it. To make things even easier, having some prepared salads ready to use also helps to keep the budget and workload in check (learn more on page 14).

3 tablespoons mirin
3 tablespoons cooking sake
3 tablespoons tamari or soy sauce
1 tablespoon brown sugar
1 tablespoon olive oil
800 g chicken thigh fillets
    (see Note 1)

TO SERVE
steamed jasmine rice
100 g edamame beans (see Note 2)
75 g (1 cup) shredded red cabbage
90 g (1 cup) julienned carrot
125 g (½ cup) whole-egg
    mayonnaise (optional)
1 teaspoon each white and black
    sesame seeds (optional)
sliced bird's eye chilli (optional)

In a bowl, make a teriyaki sauce by combining the mirin, sake, tamari or soy sauce and brown sugar. Stir well until the sugar is dissolved.

Heat the olive oil in a large frying pan over high heat and add the chicken. Cook for 8 minutes until the chicken is browned, turning once halfway through cooking.

Add the teriyaki sauce to the pan and cook for 1 minute. Turn the chicken and cook for a further 1 minute or until the sauce is caramelised and glossy.

Slice the chicken and arrange it on a bed of steamed jasmine rice. Drizzle the chicken with the pan juices. Serve with the edamame beans, red cabbage and carrot. Top with a dollop of mayonnaise and sprinkle with the sesame seeds and chilli (if using).

Singapore noodles with prawns

PREP TIME: 15 minutes

COOK TIME: 10 minutes

SERVES: 4

Note

You MUST use the standard supermarket curry powder that you buy in a tin! Ideally it should include salt as a key ingredient. Use hot or mild but don't try to use fancy curry powders with this recipe as they can be overpowering and alter the final taste of the dish.

Leftovers

Refrigerate for up to 2 days. Not suitable to freeze.

Make ahead

Prep the carrots and cabbage in advance, ready for when you need them. Learn more about food storage on page 15.

Singapore noodles are iconic, with a signature curry flavour, and traditionally made with a sticky sweet pork called char siu. This is my lighter, fresher version made with prawns and vegetables. I've gone the traditional route with cabbage and carrots but you can use any veg you like. You will be blown away by how delicious this is and how quickly you can get it on the table – the key is to prep the ingredients first. I know this is the part of preparing meals that many of us struggle with after a long day, so make sure you check out page 15 for food storage tips that will allow you to get ahead and give you back precious time and energy midweek.

250 g vermicelli rice noodles
2 tablespoons olive oil
20 raw prawns, peeled and deveined, tails intact
1 tablespoon freshly grated garlic
1 teaspoon freshly grated ginger
150 g (2 cups) finely shredded savoy cabbage
1 large carrot, peeled and julienned
2 eggs, whisked
2 spring onions, cut into 2 cm batons
chilli oil, to serve (optional)

SPICE MIX
2 tablespoons curry powder (see Note)
1 teaspoon sea salt flakes
1 teaspoon sugar
¼ teaspoon freshly ground black pepper

SAUCE
2 tablespoons tamari or soy sauce
1 tablespoon Shaoxing rice wine (Chinese cooking wine)
1 tablespoon sesame oil

Combine the spice mix ingredients in a small bowl and set aside.

Combine the sauce ingredients in a small bowl and set aside.

Cook the vermicelli rice noodles as per the packet instructions. Drain, rinse with cold water, drain again and set aside.

Heat 1 tablespoon olive oil in a large heavy-based frying pan over medium–high heat and add the prawns. Cook for 1 minute on each side, then remove them from the pan and set aside on a plate.

Add the remaining 1 tablespoon olive oil to the pan, along with the garlic and ginger and cook, stirring, for 30 seconds before adding the cabbage and carrot. Push the vegetables to one side of the pan, add the egg and cook for 1–2 minutes until set, breaking it up as you go. Combine the egg with the vegetables. Add the noodles and spring onion and return the prawns to the pan. Toss to coat.

Add the spice mix to the pan and toss to coat. Add the sauce and toss well to combine. Serve with the chilli oil (if using).

Cheat's chicken & chorizo paella

PREP TIME: 10 minutes

COOK TIME: 30 minutes

SERVES: 4

Leftovers

Refrigerate for up to 3 days. Reheat on the stovetop or in the microwave. Freeze for up to 2 months. Thaw completely in the fridge overnight before reheating (this will stop the rice turning mushy).

Spanish paella is traditionally loaded with seafood and saffron-infused rice. This quick weeknight version, all made in the one pan with super-inexpensive, accessible ingredients (no special rice or seafood is needed), is just so unbelievably delicious! We love sitting around the dinner table with a big pan of this in the centre for everyone to help themselves. The method is so simple and fuss-free, allowing us to get dinner on the table fast with minimal effort.

1 tablespoon olive oil
2 chorizo sausages (200 g total), sliced
1 onion, finely chopped
3 garlic cloves, finely chopped
300 g chicken thigh fillets, cut into bite-sized pieces
½ teaspoon sea salt flakes
½ teaspoon freshly ground black pepper
1 red capsicum, cut into strips
1 tablespoon sweet paprika
90 g crushed tomatoes or passata
440 g (2 cups) arborio rice
1 litre (4 cups) chicken stock
80 g (½ cup) frozen peas
½ bunch flat-leaf parsley, finely chopped, to serve
lemon wedges, to serve

Heat the olive oil in a large, deep, heavy-based frying pan over high heat. Add the chorizo and cook, stirring, for 2–3 minutes until the chorizo begins to release its oils and turn golden.

Add the onion, garlic, chicken, salt and pepper. Cook for 3–5 minutes, stirring occasionally, until the garlic has softened and the chicken has browned. Add the capsicum and paprika and cook for a further 2 minutes.

Add the crushed tomatoes or passata, arborio rice and chicken stock to the pan. Reduce the heat to the lowest setting, cover and cook for 15 minutes, stirring once halfway through cooking.

Add the frozen peas to the pan, place the lid back on and cook for a further 5 minutes.

Stir and leave to rest off the heat for an additional 5 minutes to absorb any residual liquid. Top with the parsley and serve with a big squeeze of lemon.

Chicken and Thai basil stir-fry with noodles

PREP TIME: 10 minutes

COOK TIME: 15 minutes

SERVES: 4

Leftovers

Refrigerate the cooked vermicelli rice noodles for up to 3 days. Refrigerate the cooked stir-fry separately for up to 3 days. Reheat the stir-fry prior to serving.

When it comes to midweek dinners, it doesn't get faster or easier than this Thai basil stir-fry. A quick soak of the rice noodles and a simple sauce made with familiar flavours are pretty much all it takes to make this a recipe my family asks for again and again. There is very little washing up, which is always welcome as it removes the pressure from dinnertime after a long day. I love a good 'catch-all' recipe that allows me to use up any vegetables that are in the fridge – carrots, sugar snap peas, mushrooms, baby corn, capsicum – although I love keeping this simple and easy with broccolini, which I always have a bunch of as it lasts so well (see page 14 for food storage tips).

200 g vermicelli rice noodles
1 tablespoon olive oil
2 spring onions, finely sliced
1 tablespoon freshly grated garlic
1 tablespoon freshly grated ginger
500 g chicken mince
1 bunch broccolini, cut into
   2 cm pieces
1 handful Thai basil (or regular
   basil), leaves picked, plus extra
   to serve
1 lime, cut into wedges

SAUCE
1 tablespoon tamari or soy sauce
1 tablespoon dark soy sauce
1 tablespoon sesame oil
1 tablespoon fish sauce
1 tablespoon brown sugar
80 ml (⅓ cup) water
2 tablespoons cornflour
½ teaspoon chicken stock powder

Combine the sauce ingredients in a bowl and mix well.

Prepare the noodles as per the packet instructions. Drain, rinse in cold water and drain again.

Heat the olive oil in a large frying pan over high heat. Add the spring onion, garlic and ginger and cook for 1 minute until fragrant. Add the chicken mince and cook for 2–3 minutes until browned, breaking it up as you go.

Add the broccolini and sauce to the pan and cook for 3 minutes until the broccolini has softened. Add the basil leaves and stir them through. Serve the chicken stir-fry on the vermicelli rice noodles with the lime wedges on the side.

Salads. Simple, fresh and ready in a matter of minutes

Spring roll salad with sticky pork & noodles

PREP TIME: 15 minutes

COOK TIME: 15 minutes

SERVES: 4

I've said it before and I'll say it again, wrapping a lettuce leaf around a spring roll and dunking it in a tangy, Vietnamese dipping sauce is everything. This salad is made with sweet, sticky pork mince together with the standard veggie spring rolls you can find in the freezer section at your local supermarket (I opt for the ones with no additives). The salad is piled high on thin rice noodles (no cooking, just a quick soak in boiling water is required) and then served with the BEST dressing. Seriously simple, fast and tasty, and a great meal to be able to make ahead too!

Note 1

The dark soy gives the pork depth of colour. You can substitute it with extra tamari or regular soy sauce. The final dish won't be a deep golden colour but it will still be delicious.

Note 2

If the dressing is too advanced for some of the eaters in your family, instead try combining equal parts tamari or soy sauce, lime juice and sweet chilli sauce.

Leftovers

Refrigerate the cooked pork for up to 3 days. Reheat in the microwave. Not suitable to freeze.

Make ahead

Prep the salads and store them refrigerated in airtight containers for when you need them. The dressing can be premade and refrigerated for up to 3 days.

Cook once, eat twice

Transform any left-over pork into pork bowls with steamed rice, sliced cucumber, tomato and a fried egg on top.

125 g vermicelli rice noodles
20 store-bought spring rolls
1 tablespoon olive oil
500 g pork mince (or chicken mince)
2 garlic cloves, finely chopped
1 tablespoon tamari or soy sauce
1 tablespoon dark soy sauce (see Note 1)

1 tablespoon rice wine vinegar
1 tablespoon brown sugar
2 gem lettuce heads, leaves removed
2 handfuls bean sprouts
2 carrots, peeled and grated or julienned
1 handful mint leaves
2 limes, halved

NUOC CHAM DRESSING
125 ml (½ cup) water
3 tablespoons fish sauce
55 g (¼ cup) sugar
3 tablespoons freshly squeezed lime juice
1 garlic clove, finely chopped
1 bird's eye chilli, deseeded and finely chopped (optional)

Cook the noodles as per the packet instructions. Drain, rinse in cold water, drain again and set aside.

Cook the spring rolls as per the packet instructions.

Heat the olive oil in a large frying pan over high heat, add the pork mince and cook for 2–3 minutes until sealed, breaking it up as you go. Add the garlic and cook, stirring, for 1 minute.Add the tamari or soy sauce, dark soy sauce, rice wine vinegar and brown sugar and cook for 5–8 minutes until caramelised and sticky. Avoid stirring too much, as this slows down the caramelisation.

Combine the nuoc cham dressing ingredients in a bowl and set aside.

Divide the noodles, cooked pork, spring rolls, lettuce leaves, bean sprouts, carrot, mint and lime halves among four bowls. Dress each bowl generously with the dressing and serve.

Creamy potato salad

PREP TIME: 15 minutes

COOK TIME: 10 minutes

SERVES: 4

Leftovers

Store leftovers refrigerated for up to 2 days. The potatoes will absorb the dressing and the salad will become less creamy, but the taste will still be delicious.

Make ahead

Prepare the salad ingredients and dressing. Store separately and refrigerate for up to 2 days. Combine the salad ingredients with the dressing when ready to serve.

Potato salad is one of my all-time favourite sides and I make it at least once a week, year-round – even more in the summer months. It's creamy and comforting and complements so many dishes, especially with fresh bread rolls and something hot off the barbecue. I steam the potatoes in the microwave, which gives my kitchen a little breathing space with no big pans cluttering the stovetop (great for when entertaining). It can be served warm or made in advance and served cold. The dressing is just beautiful, made with dill, tangy capers and pickles. There are so many variations of potato salad and yet I'm constantly drawn to this one – it is that good!

8 all-purpose potatoes (I normally factor in 2 potatoes per person), scrubbed

DRESSING
90 g (⅓ cup) whole-egg mayonnaise
1 tablespoon olive oil
1 tablespoon apple cider vinegar
1 tablespoon roughly chopped capers

1 tablespoon finely chopped pickles
¼ red onion, finely chopped
1 tablespoon finely chopped dill sprigs (optional)
½ teaspoon sea salt flakes
½ teaspoon freshly ground black pepper

Cook the potatoes, microwave method: Place the whole potatoes (skin on) and 125 ml (½ cup) water in a large, microwave-safe container. Place the lid slightly ajar and cook in the microwave on High for 10 minutes. When cooked, you should easily be able to pierce the potatoes with a fork. If firm, continue cooking in 2-minute intervals. Once cooked, drain and allow to cool for 5–10 minutes before handling.

Cook the potatoes, stovetop method: Place the potatoes in a large saucepan and add water to cover them by at least 5 cm. Bring to the boil, then simmer for 20–25 minutes until they can be easily pierced with a fork. Drain and allow to cool for 5–10 minutes before handling.

Peel the skin off the potatoes using your fingers and a butter knife. It will peel off easily. Cut the potatoes into bite-sized pieces – they may crumble a little, and that's okay.

Combine the dressing ingredients in a large bowl. Add the potatoes and toss them to coat in the dressing. Serve warm.

Chicken salad with creamy peanut dressing

PREP TIME: 15 minutes

COOK TIME: nil

SERVES: 4

Note 1

You can substitute the sweet chilli sauce for honey or maple syrup. If you would like more of a chilli hit, add 1 teaspoon sriracha.

Note 2

Use rice wine vinegar, white vinegar or apple cider vinegar as a lime juice substitute.

Leftovers

Once combined with the dressing, the salad is best served and eaten immediately as the veggies start to soften. However, leftovers can be stored in an airtight container and consumed within 24 hours.

Make ahead

Prepare the salad ingredients and dressing and refrigerate, stored separately, for up to 3 days. Dress the salad just before serving.

A big focus for our family is ensuring there is no waste, and the best way for me to manage that is to take a bit of time once the groceries arrive to wash and prep my vegetables (learn more on page 14). This incredible salad is one that I have been making for years. I decided to share it on social media and my little salad received millions of views. The creamy peanut dressing is incredibly delicious yet so simple to make and the salad can be made ahead – perfect for work lunches or picnics.

500 g poached chicken or left-over roast chicken (page 54)
150 g (2 cups) shredded green cabbage
150 g (2 cups) shredded red cabbage
2 cups shredded carrot
2 Lebanese cucumbers, sliced
200 g frozen edamame beans, thawed
2 tablespoons fried shallots (optional)
2 tablespoons sesame seeds (optional)

CREAMY PEANUT DRESSING

60 g (¼ cup) natural smooth peanut butter
3 tablespoons tamari or soy sauce
3 tablespoons sweet chilli sauce (see Note 1)
3 tablespoons freshly squeezed lime juice (see Note 2)
3 tablespoons warm water
2 tablespoons sesame oil

Combine the chicken, cabbages, carrot, cucumber and edamame beans in a large bowl.

Combine the creamy peanut dressing ingredients in another bowl – use extra warm water if needed to thin the dressing to your liking.

Drizzle the dressing over the salad and toss to combine. Divide among four bowls, top with the fried shallots and sesame seeds (if using) and serve.

Tuna bowl with miso dressing

PREP TIME: 20 minutes

COOK TIME: nil

SERVES: 4

Leftovers

Best made and eaten immediately but leftovers can be stored in the fridge for up to 24 hours.

Make ahead

All components of the salad can be made and refrigerated for up to 3 days. Store the dressing, noodles, salads and tuna mixture in separate airtight containers. See the food storage tips on page 15 for more information.

My kids would eat this tuna bowl every single day if I let them. The miso dressing takes an otherwise ordinary protein and transforms it into something amazing. This is a fantastic meal to prep in advance (see more information on page 15) and have ready for when you need it. It's veg-forward and can be made with whatever you have on hand, but for me it's the little pops of edamame beans and pickled ginger (both widely available at major supermarkets) that make it extra special. Miso paste can be found at all major supermarkets and most pastes last for up to 3 months in the fridge. Aside from using it in this dressing, it can also be used in marinades or simply stirred into hot water to make a quick miso soup. It's a staple at our place and definitely something worth adding to your weekly grocery shop if you haven't tried it before.

250 g soba noodles
400 g canned tuna, drained
60 g (¼ cup) whole-egg mayonnaise
100 g (½ cup) canned corn kernels, rinsed and drained
2 Lebanese cucumbers, sliced
100 g frozen edamame beans, thawed
90 g (1 cup) julienned carrot
75 g (1 cup) shredded red cabbage
1 avocado, sliced
pickled ginger, to serve
1 teaspoon mixed black and white sesame seeds, to serve

MISO DRESSING

2 tablespoons rice wine vinegar
1 tablespoon miso paste (white or red)
1 tablespoon tamari or soy sauce
1 teaspoon brown sugar
1 teaspoon sesame seeds

Combine the miso dressing ingredients in a small bowl and set aside.

Prepare the soba noodles as per the packet instructions. Drain, rinse with cold water, drain again and set aside.

Combine the tuna, mayonnaise and corn in a bowl, mixing well.

Divide the soba noodles among four bowls. Top with the cucumber, edamame beans, carrot, red cabbage and avocado. Drizzle with the dressing.

Divide the tuna mixture among the four bowls. Top with the pickled ginger, sprinkle with the sesame seeds and serve.

Chicken caesar with bacon & croutons

PREP TIME: 15 minutes

COOK TIME: 15 minutes

SERVES: 4

Leftovers

Once dressed, chicken caesar salad is best eaten immediately.

Make ahead

Cooked chicken Can be refrigerated for up to 3 days. Serve warm or cold.

Bacon Can be refrigerated for up to 3 days (some of the fat will solidify; reheat it in a 200°C fan-forced oven for 5 minutes until warmed through).

Croutons Store in an airtight container for up to 3 days.

Dressing Store refrigerated in an airtight container for up to 2 days.

Cos lettuce See food storage instructions page 15.

Cook once, eat twice

Stuff the chicken caesar into a wrap or make extra chicken to serve in sandwiches or other salads, such as the Chicken Salad with Creamy Peanut Dressing (page 123).

I love a good little shortcut in the kitchen, but one thing you won't catch me buying is bottled salad dressing. Aside from the outrageous flavour pay-off I get from making my own, the ability to control my ingredients and save on waste (no half-opened bottles in the fridge!), it is SO easy to make. Homemade caesar salad may seem like a lot of effort but I have refined this recipe over the years so that it's achievable and quick. The bacon and croutons are toasted simultaneously in the oven and the chicken is perfect for meal-prep days, lasting in the fridge for up to 3 days and versatile enough to be used in any salad recipe.

SALAD
200 g streaky bacon
4 slices sourdough bread, torn into bite-sized pieces
olive oil spray
½ teaspoon sea salt flakes
2 cos lettuce hearts, cut into bite-sized pieces
25 g (¼ cup) freshly grated parmesan

CHICKEN
2 chicken breast fillets, cut in half horizontally to make 4 steaks
1 teaspoon sweet paprika
1 teaspoon sea salt flakes
½ teaspoon freshly ground black pepper
2 tablespoons olive oil

CAESAR DRESSING
250 g (1 cup) whole-egg mayonnaise
2 tablespoons olive oil
½ teaspoon freshly grated garlic
2 anchovy fillets, finely chopped (optional)
1 tablespoon freshly squeezed lemon juice
1 teaspoon dijon mustard
1 teaspoon Worcester-shire sauce
25 g (¼ cup) freshly grated parmesan
½ teaspoon sea salt flakes
¼ teaspoon freshly ground black pepper

Preheat the oven to 200°C fan-forced. Line two baking trays with baking paper.

For the salad, place the bacon on one of the trays, taking care to not overlap. Place the sourdough pieces on the other tray, spray generously with olive oil and sprinkle with salt. Place the bacon on the top rack of the oven and the sourdough croutons on the bottom rack. Cook the bacon for 12–15 minutes until crispy. Cook the sourdough croutons for 8–10 minutes until golden. Set aside.

Once the bacon is cool, cut it into bite-sized pieces and set aside.

Meanwhile, for the chicken, in a large shallow dish, sprinkle the chicken breast with the paprika, salt and pepper. Drizzle with the olive oil and use your hands to coat evenly.

Heat a large frying pan over medium heat and cook the chicken for 6–8 minutes until golden and cooked, turning once halfway through. Add 2 tablespoons water in the last 2 minutes of cooking and stir to deglaze the pan – it will create a lovely coating over the chicken. Slice the chicken into thin strips and set aside.

For the caesar dressing, combine all the ingredients in a large shallow bowl.

Add the cos lettuce directly to the dressing and toss to combine. Top with the chicken, bacon and sourdough croutons. Sprinkle with the parmesan and serve.

Thai beef & noodle salad

PREP TIME: 15 minutes

COOK TIME: 10 minutes

SERVES: 4

Leftovers

Refrigerate for up to 24 hours (the herbs will darken so it's best made and eaten immediately). Not suitable to freeze.

Make ahead

Prepare the salad, noodles, dressing and beef mince up to 3 days in advance. Refrigerate the components in separate containers. Check out the food storage tips on page 15 for more information.

This salad is uncomplicated cooking at its best. Prepare the ingredients, have them ready in the fridge and you've got an easy dinner or lunch that comes together in less than 2 minutes. The zingy dressing is paired with fragrant herbs and rice noodles (which only take a few minutes to soak). It is just so delicious! This recipe uses beef mince instead of classic beef strips and – dare I say – I like this version better. It comes together quickly (the beef mince takes mere minutes to cook) and the sweet and salty beef distributes throughout the salad so every mouthful is filled with flavour. It's the perfect meal to make when you feel like something summery and fresh or if you're feeding a crowd.

250 g vermicelli rice noodles
1 tablespoon olive oil
500 g beef mince
1 teaspoon freshly grated ginger
1 teaspoon freshly grated garlic
2 tablespoons tamari or soy sauce
2 tablespoons runny honey
2 tablespoons freshly squeezed
  lime juice
2 large cucumbers, sliced
250 g cherry tomatoes, quartered
½ red onion, finely sliced
½ bunch Thai basil, leaves picked
½ bunch coriander, leaves picked
½ bunch mint, leaves picked
35 g (¼ cup) crushed peanuts
40 g fried shallots

DRESSING

3 tablespoons freshly squeezed lime
  juice or rice wine vinegar
2 tablespoons brown sugar
1 tablespoon tamari or soy sauce
1 tablespoon fish sauce
1 tablespoon sesame oil
¼ teaspoon freshly grated garlic
¼ teaspoon freshly grated ginger

Combine the dressing ingredients with 2 tablespoons water in a small jug and set aside.

Prepare the vermicelli rice noodles as per the packet instructions. Drain, rinse under cold water, drain again and set aside.

Heat the olive oil in a large heavy-based frying pan over medium–high heat and add the beef mince. Flatten the mince without breaking it up and cook for 2–3 minutes. Flip and cook for a further 2 minutes before breaking it up with a wooden spoon (this method allows the beef to get crispy quickly). Add the ginger and garlic and cook, stirring, for 30 seconds. Add the tamari or soy sauce, honey and lime juice and cook for 1 minute until slightly caramelised.

Divide the vermicelli rice noodles among four bowls. Divide the cucumber, cherry tomatoes, red onion and herbs among the bowls and drizzle with the dressing. Top with the beef mince, crushed peanuts and fried shallots and serve.

Beetroot, feta & wild rice salad

PREP TIME: 5 minutes

COOK TIME: nil

SERVES: 8

This is my go-to salad when I'm entertaining. It looks super fancy and special, yet 5 minutes is all it takes and no cooking is required. It's all thanks to a few clever supermarket purchases. I put this on the table and always feel pretty happy with myself, knowing I haven't done much more than cut up an onion. You will love this sweet and tangy, vibrant salad with earthy beetroot, peppery rocket, Persian feta and wild rice, and it pretty much goes with everything.

2 × 250 g packets microwave brown, red and wild rice medley (see Note)
120 g baby rocket leaves
500 g cooked, peeled beetroot, quartered (or canned beetroot)
½ red onion, finely sliced
35 g (⅓ cup) walnuts, toasted
50 g (⅓ cup) crumbled Persian feta

DRESSING
juice of 1 lemon
3 tablespoons olive oil
1 tablespoon runny honey
1 teaspoon dijon mustard
½ teaspoon sea salt flakes
½ teaspoon freshly ground black pepper

Prepare the wild rice according to the packet instructions.

Spread the rice out evenly on a large platter and top it with the rocket, beetroot, onion, walnuts and feta.

Combine the dressing ingredients in a bowl, then drizzle the dressing over the salad. Toss to coat.

Serve the salad at room temperature or refrigerate and serve cold.

Note

You can use any variety of rice you like. You need the equivalent of 2 cups cooked rice (either freshly made or microwave rice). I recommend brown rice as it's slightly more earthy and nutty, which pairs beautifully with the beetroot.

Leftovers

Best eaten immediately but leftovers can be stored in the fridge for up to 24 hours.

Slow. Take your time with these slow show stoppers

Toasty roasted pumpkin soup

PREP TIME: 10 minutes

COOK TIME: 1 hour
40 minutes

SERVES: 4–6

Note 1

The garlic skins must be left on. If they are peeled, they will burn. By cutting off the tops you can squeeze the flesh out of the garlic bulb at the end of the cooking time directly into your soup before blending.

Note 2

If the pumpkin is still hard at the end of 1½ hours, roast it, covered, in 20-minute intervals until soft.

Leftovers

Refrigerate for up to 3 days. Freeze for up to 3 months. Thaw completely overnight in the fridge. Reheat on the stovetop or in the microwave.

The comfort of a delicious pumpkin soup is one thing, but actually taking the time out of your day to prepare it is another. This method of roasting butternut pumpkin halves and scooping out the gloriously soft flesh revolutionised pumpkin soup for me. You do not have to peel or cut up the butternut pumpkin – this alone is enough for this recipe to be a winner and encourages me to actually make it! In 10 minutes, you'll have the makings of the best pumpkin soup you'll ever eat, with a deep, toasty flavour. This makes a generous batch, perfect for freezing and eating later. I like to top mine with a dollop of sour cream, some finely chopped chives and chilli flakes and serve it with crusty sourdough bread or a big chunk of freezer-friendly garlic bread (page 86). I know I won't be able to eat regular pumpkin soup ever again!

2 butternut pumpkins, halved lengthways, seeds removed
2 large onions, halved
2 whole garlic bulbs, skin on, tops sliced off (see Note 1)
80 ml (⅓ cup) olive oil
1 teaspoon sea salt flakes, plus extra

1 teaspoon freshly ground black pepper, plus extra
1 litre (4 cups) chicken stock (at room temperature)
sour cream, to serve (optional)
chives, finely chopped, to serve (optional)
chilli flakes, to serve (optional)
sourdough bread, sliced, to serve

Preheat the oven to 180°C fan-forced.

Arrange the pumpkin, onion and garlic on a deep baking tray. Drizzle with the olive oil and sprinkle with the salt and pepper.

Roast for 45 minutes. Add 125 ml (½ cup) water and cover with foil – this will ensure the vegetables don't burn and speed up the cooking time (see Note 2). Roast for a further 45 minutes or until the pumpkin is soft enough to be pierced easily with a fork.

Once the vegetables have cooled slightly, use your fingers to squeeze the garlic flesh from its skin. Scoop the pumpkin flesh out of its skin with a spoon and transfer to a large stockpot on the stovetop with the cooked onion and garlic.

Add the chicken stock to the pot and blend to your desired consistency using a hand-held blender. Heat the soup on medium–high heat and simmer until it is warmed through.

Season the soup with extra salt and pepper, top with the sour cream, chives and chilli flakes (if using) and serve with the sourdough bread on the side.

Rich red wine & tomato beef ragu

PREP TIME: 10 minutes

COOK TIME: 2 hours 45 minutes

SERVES: 6–8

Note

If the beef is still tough after 2½ hours of cooking, it needs to cook for longer. Make sure the sauce is bubbling gently (you should still be able to see bubbles appearing in the sauce – if not, the heat is too low and the beef will take a lot longer to cook). The beauty of chuck steak is that it is almost impossible to overcook. The longer it cooks, the more it will soften and break down into the sauce. Continue cooking in 30-minute intervals; if the sauce seems to be too thick and sticking to the base of the pan, add 125 ml (½ cup) water.

Leftovers

Refrigerate for up to 3 days. Freeze for up to 3 months. Thaw completely overnight in the fridge before reheating on the stove top or in the microwave.

I am a massive fan of one-pot recipes as they mean less washing up, which I always appreciate! But this one is extra special. Beef ragu has a wow-factor. Beef is slowly cooked in a luscious tomato and red wine–based sauce before being piled on top of pasta and sprinkled with (a lot!) of parmesan. The best part about this dish is that there are no complicated instructions or specialty ingredients needed. I choose to make this on days where I'm pottering around the house. I can put this on and have it blipping away in the background and then come back to a big, delicious bowl of comfort. An added bonus is that this beef ragu can be made in bulk and frozen in batches, ready for whenever it is needed.

2 tablespoons olive oil
2 onions, finely diced
2 large carrots, peeled and finely diced
2 celery stalks, finely diced
2 garlic cloves, roughly chopped
800 g–1 kg chuck steak, cut into roughly 2 cm cubes
125 ml (½ cup) red wine
125 g (½ cup) tomato paste
700 g jar passata
500 ml (2 cups) beef stock
1 teaspoon sea salt flakes
½ teaspoon freshly ground black pepper
1 teaspoon dried thyme
2 bay leaves
cooked pasta of your choice, to serve
freshly grated parmesan, to serve

Heat the olive oil in a deep heavy-based frying pan with a lid over medium–high heat. Add the onion, carrot, celery and garlic and cook, stirring, for 3–5 minutes until softened.

Increase the heat to high, add the beef and cook, stirring, for 2–3 minutes until browned. Add the red wine, tomato paste, passata, beef stock, salt, pepper, thyme and bay leaves and stir them through.

Bring the ragu to a simmer, then cover and reduce the heat to the lowest setting. Cook for 2½ hours or until the beef is tender enough to be easily shredded with two forks (see Note). Shred the beef and serve with your favourite cooked pasta and the parmesan.

Outrageously crispy buttermilk fried chicken

PREP TIME: 10 minutes

COOK TIME: 30 minutes

SERVES: 4

This isn't a meal we eat every day but, when the mood strikes, there is nothing better than this buttermilk fried chicken. It's the ultimate comfort food, which can be made at home with simple, recognisable, inexpensive ingredients.

1.2 kg chicken pieces (see Note 1)
375 ml (1½ cups) buttermilk (see Note 2)
1 egg, whisked
1 teaspoon sea salt flakes
oil, for frying (see Note 3)
gherkins, to serve

CHICKEN COATING
150 g (1 cup) plain flour
125 g (1 cup) cornflour
2 teaspoons sea salt flakes
2 teaspoons sweet paprika
2 teaspoons garlic powder
1 teaspoon onion powder

'EVERYTHING' COLESLAW
150 g (2 cups) shredded green cabbage
150 g (2 cups) shredded red cabbage
1 large carrot, peeled and julienned
2 spring onions, finely sliced
60 g (⅔ cup) whole-egg mayonnaise
1 tablespoon apple cider vinegar
1 tablespoon olive oil
1 teaspoon sea salt flakes
¼ teaspoon freshly ground black pepper

Leftovers

Chicken Refrigerate for up to 3 days. Reheat in a preheated 200°C fan-forced oven for 10 minutes or until heated through. Not suitable to freeze.

Coleslaw Refrigerate dressed coleslaw for up to 24 hours.

Make ahead

Chicken Marinate the chicken in the buttermilk mixture for up to 24 hours prior to coating in the flour. Leave it out on the counter to come to room temperature for 20 minutes before coating and cooking. Once coated in the flour, it needs to be cooked immediately.

Coleslaw Check out the food storage tips on page 15 if you want to get ahead and prepare your coleslaw in advance. The dressing can be refrigerated separately for up to 3 days.

Place the chicken, buttermilk, egg and salt in a bowl and toss to coat.

Combine the chicken coating ingredients on a large piece of baking paper.

Remove the chicken from the marinade, a piece at a time, letting any excess marinade drip off. Dredge the chicken in the coating mixture, pressing to cover in the crumbs. Once the chicken pieces are coated, cook them immediately.

Preheat the oven to 100°C fan-forced.

Heat the oil in a large, heavy-based frying pan over medium heat. Working in batches, use tongs to place the chicken pieces in the oil and, once in the pan, try not to move the chicken around for the first 2–3 minutes as the coating will fall off. Do not overcrowd the pan as the drop in temperature will affect the crispiness. Cook bone-in chicken pieces for 14–16 minutes and boneless chicken pieces for 8–10 minutes, turning once halfway through cooking.

Transfer the chicken pieces to a wire rack and keep them warm in the oven while you cook the rest, or allow the chicken to drain on a plate lined with paper towel.

To make the coleslaw, combine the ingredients in a bowl and toss to coat.

Serve the chicken with the coleslaw and gherkins.

Note 1

Chicken thigh cutlets, wings, drumsticks (skin on or off) or thigh fillets all work for this recipe, but I like to buy a whole free-range chicken (1.2 –1.8 kg) and cut it into pieces myself. There are loads of videos on the internet to show you how to do this. I remove the breasts to make schnitzels, then fry the wings, drumsticks and thigh cutlets whole. This is the best option from a budget perspective, and the end result is more flavourful, tender and faster to cook.

Note 2

If you don't have buttermilk, combine 375 ml (1½ cups) of milk with 1 tablespoon freshly squeezed lemon juice, then set the mixture aside for 5 minutes before using. (It will curdle, which is fine.)

Note 3

A high smoke point oil (e.g. canola, vegetable or sunflower oil) is best for this recipe. It needs to be at least 3 cm deep in the pan.

Asian-style braised sticky soy pork belly

PREP TIME: 15 minutes

COOK TIME: 2 hours 45 minutes

SERVES: 4–6

Leftovers

Refrigerate for up to 3 days. Freeze for up to 2 months, ensuring the pork is well covered in the sticky broth to prevent freezer burn. Best thawed completely overnight in the fridge before use. Reheat in the microwave or on the stovetop with a splash of boiling water to help loosen the sauce.

Cook once, eat twice

Stuff left-over pork into bao buns with sriracha mayo, shredded cabbage and grated carrot.

Eating out really slowed down for my husband and me once the kids were born, for so many reasons. We found ourselves desiring to eat out less (hello exhaustion), we became more mindful about what was in the food we were eating, and we were also happy to save money where we could. This Asian-style braised pork belly is the type of dish we used to eat out because it seemed too intimidating to make at home. However, one day a craving set in and I wowed myself with how simple it was to make melt-in-the-mouth, slow-cooked pork belly in a thick, sticky glaze, all in the comfort of my own home. I have now made this dish countless times and serve it with steamed rice and steamed greens with a hint of fresh chilli to top it off. On the rare occasion that we have leftovers, they can be refrigerated or frozen.

1 tablespoon olive oil
1 kg pork belly, cut into 2–3 cm cubes (you can use up to 1.5 kg pork belly for this recipe)
1 whole garlic bulb, cloves broken off, peeled and roughly chopped
3 red onions, roughly sliced (brown onions are fine too)
1 thumb-sized piece of ginger, peeled and cut into thin matchsticks

95 g (½ cup) brown sugar
125 ml (½ cup) tamari or soy sauce
1 teaspoon Chinese five-spice
2 star anise
sliced bird's eye chilli (optional)
steamed jasmine rice, to serve
steamed greens, to serve

Heat the olive oil in a large frying pan over medium–high heat and cook the pork belly in batches for 5–8 minutes until browned and golden. Remove the pork from the pan and set aside.

Add the garlic, onion and ginger to the same pan and cook for 2–3 minutes until slightly softened and fragrant. Don't worry if you haven't cut the ingredients too finely; they will break down in the delicious, sticky sauce.

Add the brown sugar, tamari or soy sauce, Chinese five-spice, star anise and 500 ml (2 cups) water to the pan. Return the pork to the pan and bring to a simmer. Reduce the heat to the lowest setting, cover and cook for 2 hours. Check halfway through cooking and add 125 ml (½ cup) water if the sauce is sticking to the base of the pan. The sauce will be thin during the cooking process, but will caramelise and thicken in the last 10 minutes of cooking time.

Once cooked, the pork should easily break apart with a fork. If not, cook in 15-minute intervals until soft, adding up to 3 tablespoons of water as needed.

Once the pork is tender, remove the lid, and increase the heat to high for 5–10 minutes to let the sauce thicken. It is ready when the sauce is sticky and coats the pork. Sprinkle on the chilli (if using) and serve with some steamed rice and steamed greens.

Glazed barbecue brisket with mac & cheese

PREP TIME: 20 minutes

COOK TIME: 10 hours 15 minutes

SERVES: 6

Leftovers

Refrigerate the brisket for up to 3 days. Refrigerate the mac and cheese for up to 3 days or freeze for up to 2 months – thaw completely in the fridge overnight before reheating.

Make ahead

Brisket Once the brisket is cooked in the slow cooker, transfer it along with the (unreduced) liquid to a roasting tin. Cover and refrigerate for up to 3 days. Bake, covered with foil, in a 180°C fan-forced oven for 30 minutes until warmed through. Uncover and grill for 5 minutes or until the sauce thickens. Although some recipes state otherwise, brisket isn't my favourite to freeze, as I find it a little dry when reheated. But if you choose to freeze it (up to 2 months, covered in as much sauce as possible), make sure you thaw it completely in the fridge overnight before reheating.

Each week I make a conscious effort to get the family involved in meal planning. Nine times out of ten, my husband will quickly respond: 'Your brisket'. Brisket has become pretty popular in the last few years, and there aren't many pub menus that don't include some sort of brisket in a smoky barbecue sauce. What's exciting is that this amazing, inexpensive cut of beef is now easy to find at the supermarket. It transforms into tender, delicious slices in the slow cooker that can be served with coleslaw heaped on brioche buns or with mac and cheese. I compared the cost of this meal at my local pub and one serving was almost the same price as all the ingredients for this recipe that serves six. This brisket is definitely worth the effort, and I use the term 'effort' lightly because it's a simple recipe to prepare, much of which can be made ahead of time.

800 g–1 kg beef brisket
2 teaspoons sea salt flakes
1 tablespoon olive oil
'Everything Coleslaw' (page 139), to serve

BARBECUE SAUCE
250 g (1 cup) ketchup
3 tablespoons apple cider vinegar
60 g (⅓ cup) brown sugar
1 tablespoon dijon mustard
1 tablespoon Worcestershire sauce
1 tablespoon ground cumin
1 tablespoon sweet paprika
1 tablespoon onion powder

1 tablespoon garlic powder
1 teaspoon sea salt flakes
250 ml (1 cup) beef stock

MAC AND CHEESE
250 g elbow pasta
60 g unsalted butter
35 g (¼ cup) plain flour
750 ml (3 cups) full-cream milk
250 g (2 cups) freshly grated tasty cheese
1 teaspoon chicken stock powder
1 teaspoon sea salt flakes
20 g (⅓ cup) panko breadcrumbs
olive oil spray

Sprinkle the brisket with salt on all sides. Heat the olive oil in a large, heavy-based frying pan over medium–high heat, add the brisket and cook for 3–4 minutes or until it is browned all over. Set aside.

Combine all the barbecue sauce ingredients in a jug and stir well.

Transfer the beef to a slow cooker (squish it in if you need to) and pour the sauce over the top so that the beef is covered. Cook on low for 8–10 hours or on high for 4–5 hours until the beef is tender.

Remove the beef from the slow cooker and slice.

Transfer the sauce to a large saucepan (the wider the surface area, the more quickly the sauce will thicken!) and simmer over medium–high heat for 4–5 minutes until thickened. Drizzle the sauce over the cooked brisket.

Meanwhile, for the mac and cheese, cook the pasta as per the packet instructions minus 1 minute. Drain and set aside.

Preheat the oven grill.

Heat the butter in a large frying pan over medium–high heat and, once melted, add the flour. Cook, stirring, for 1 minute to form a paste. Slowly add the milk, whisking constantly for 5 minutes until the sauce is thick enough to coat the back of a spoon. Add the cheese, chicken stock powder, salt and cooked pasta and stir them through. Top with the breadcrumbs and spray with the olive oil. Grill for 2 minutes until the top is golden and crispy.

Serve the brisket with the mac and cheese and coleslaw.

Fragrant chicken noodle soup

PREP TIME: 10 minutes

COOK TIME: 1 hour
45 minutes

SERVES: 4

Note

You will need ¾ teaspoon sea salt flakes per 1 litre (4 cups) water. The amount of water you use will depend on the size of your pot. Ensure the chicken is completely submerged in the water. If you are using regular table salt, use ½ teaspoon salt per 1 litre (4 cups) water.

Leftovers

Can be refrigerated for up to 3 days, although the noodles will absorb the liquid as the soup sits. Reheat in the microwave or on the stovetop. Freeze for up to 3 months. Follow the recipe but do not add the egg noodles. Thaw in the fridge overnight. Reheat on the stovetop, then add the egg noodles and cook for 10 minutes. This will stop the noodles absorbing all the liquid. Add store-bought chicken stock or boiling water to loosen if required.

Cook once, eat twice

I often shred the entire chicken for the soup but you can reserve the chicken breasts for poached chicken and mayo sandwiches or Chicken Salad with Creamy Peanut Dressing (page 123).

Growing up, there was always a pot of this chicken soup simmering on the stove. When I made it for the first time, I had my mum on speed dial, walking me through every step. It's a simple dish, full of goodness, made with a whole chicken and vegetables, which slowly cook until they are tender and fragrant in a golden, nutrient-filled broth. I whip this recipe out whenever anyone in the family needs a boost of energy or simply when I'm feeling like I need comfort. One chicken goes such a long way. Don't be put off by the cooking time, as the prep is so easy and you can make a big batch to freeze.

2 tablespoons olive oil
2 onions, finely diced
1 whole chicken (1.2–1.8 kg)
2 large carrots, peeled and halved lengthways
2 celery stalks, including leaves, cut into 15 cm lengths (so they are small enough to fit in the pot)
3 teaspoons sea salt flakes
1 teaspoon freshly ground black pepper, plus extra to serve
1 tablespoon apple cider vinegar
3–4 litres filtered water
100 g vermicelli egg noodles
2 tablespoons finely chopped flat-leaf parsley
crusty bread, to serve

Heat the olive oil in a stockpot (large enough to fit the chicken) over medium heat and cook the onion for 3–5 minutes until soft.

Rinse the chicken inside and out (this creates a clearer broth).

Place the whole chicken in the pot, along with the carrot, celery, salt, pepper, apple cider vinegar and filtered water – you will need enough water to just cover the chicken (see Note). Bring to the boil, then reduce the heat to a gentle simmer. Cover, with the lid slightly ajar, and cook for 1½ hours or until the chicken is tender and falling off the bone. The liquid should reduce by a quarter and you should be left with a deep golden broth. If not, continue cooking in 20-minute intervals.

Using tongs, remove the chicken, carrot and celery from the broth and set aside on a plate. (You can strain the broth if you wish using a sieve. It will produce a clearer broth, but the flavour of the soup will not change so you can skip this step.)

Shred the chicken and cut the carrot and celery into bite-sized pieces.

Add the vermicelli egg noodles to the broth and cook for 10 minutes. Return the chicken, carrot and celery to the soup. Discard the celery leaves.

Serve the soup topped with parsley, an extra sprinkling of black pepper and some crusty bread.

Panang coconut & peanut beef curry

PREP TIME: 15 minutes

COOK TIME: 3 hours
20 minutes

SERVES: 6

Leftovers

Refrigerate for up to 2 days. Freeze for up to 2 months. Thaw completely in the fridge overnight before reheating.

I was 20 when I had my first curry, made by my then boyfriend's (now husband's) mum. I had grown up eating traditional Eastern European food and hadn't really been exposed to different cuisines up until that point. I was amazed by the flavours of the curry and I have made hundreds of curries since, experimenting with different flavours and proteins. Marrying my husband saw the merging of two very different cultures and it was such a beautiful moment seeing my traditional European parents be so accepting and open to trying new foods, too. Mum now requests a curry on her birthday every year. Panang curry is a type of Thai red curry with a signature peanut flavour and, aside from being deliciously warm, cosy and filling, it is incredibly easy to make. It's the perfect meal to have simmering on your stovetop on a rainy day. I choose 'safe' vegetables that I know my family enjoy, but you can add any veggies you like.

1 tablespoon olive oil
1 kg chuck steak, cut into
   approximately 2 cm cubes
200 g panang curry paste
60 g (¼ cup) natural smooth
   peanut butter
400 ml can coconut milk
2 tablespoons fish sauce
1 tablespoon brown sugar
1 tablespoon rice wine vinegar
4 fresh makrut lime leaves (optional)

375 ml (1½ cups) beef stock
200 g green beans, trimmed
   and halved
1 red capsicum, finely sliced
1 handful Thai basil leaves
   (or regular basil)
40 g (¼ cup) crushed peanuts,
   to serve
steamed jasmine rice sprinkled
   with fried shallots, to serve
lime wedges, to serve (optional)

Heat the olive oil in a large heavy-based frying pan over medium–high heat. Cook the beef in batches for 2–3 minutes until browned on all sides. Remove the beef from the pan and set aside on a plate.

Add the curry paste, peanut butter, coconut milk, fish sauce, brown sugar, rice wine vinegar, makrut lime leaves (if using) and beef stock to the same pan. Stir well, bring to the boil, then reduce the heat to the lowest setting. Cook, covered, for 2½ hours, stirring once every hour. Add 125 ml (½ cup) water if the sauce is starting to stick to the base of the pan.

Uncover and cook for a further 30 minutes or until the beef is fork tender. Add the green beans, capsicum and Thai basil (reserving a few leaves to serve) and cook for a further 5 minutes.

Scatter on the reserved basil leaves, top with the crushed peanuts and a squeeze of lime (if using) and serve with jasmine rice topped with fried shallots.

Goulash with creamy polenta & cabbage

PREP TIME: 15 minutes

COOK TIME: 3 hours

SERVES: 4

Note

Pork shoulder is an inexpensive cut of meat that is found at most major supermarkets. I usually buy a 2 kg piece and use half for this recipe and freeze the rest. A suitable alternative is pork scotch fillet. Cut it into bite-sized pieces and use as per the recipe.

Goulash, complete with creamy polenta and braised cabbage, tastes like home to me. There are so many variations of this comforting stew from different regions, but my favourite version is this one, slightly different from the way my mum makes it. Pork shoulder is simmered until tender with paprika and vegetables that melt into a flavour-packed gravy, before being topped with a big dollop of sour cream. The sweet-and-sour braised cabbage is the perfect accompaniment, which transports me to Central Europe every time I eat it, and the polenta is one of the easiest and fastest sides to make as well as being so deliciously creamy when laced with parmesan. This goulash is a simple and restorative meal that requires very little preparation and can be made in bulk and frozen, which is always a win.

800 g pork shoulder, rind removed, cut into bite-sized pieces (see Note)
1 teaspoon sea salt flakes
½ teaspoon freshly ground black pepper
2 tablespoons olive oil
1 teaspoon finely chopped garlic
2 onions, roughly diced
1 large carrot, peeled and roughly diced
1 celery stalk, roughly diced
2 tablespoons sweet paprika
1 teaspoon caraway seeds (optional)
2 tablespoons tomato paste
2 tablespoons plain flour
500 ml (2 cups) beef stock
sour cream, to serve
flat-leaf parsley, finely chopped, to serve (optional)

BRAISED RED CABBAGE

1 tablespoon olive oil
1 large onion, finely diced
1 green apple, peeled and grated
½ large red cabbage, finely shredded
80 ml (⅓ cup) apple cider vinegar
1 teaspoon sea salt flakes
1 tablespoon brown sugar
½ teaspoon freshly ground black pepper
85 g (⅔ cup) sultanas

CREAMY POLENTA

500 ml (2 cups) full-cream milk
250 g instant polenta
40 g butter
50 g (½ cup) freshly grated parmesan
1½ teaspoons sea salt flakes

Leftovers

Refrigerate cooked goulash for up to 3 days or freeze for up to 3 months. Thaw completely overnight in the fridge before use. Reheat in the microwave or on the stovetop. Refrigerate cooked braised red cabbage separately for up to 3 days. Freeze for up to 3 months. Refrigerate cooked polenta for up to 3 days (it will become firmer in texture but equally delicious to eat).

Cook once, eat twice

Transform left-over polenta into polenta chips! Refrigerate leftovers overnight in a rectangular container, then cut the chilled polenta into chips. Lay the polenta chips on a baking tray lined with baking paper, spray all over with olive oil, sprinkle with a dusting of extra uncooked polenta and sea salt flakes, then bake in a 200°C fan-forced oven for 30 minutes until crisp and golden.

Place the pork in a bowl. Sprinkle the pork with salt and pepper and toss to coat, using tongs.

Heat 1 tablespoon olive oil in a large, heavy-based frying pan over high heat and cook the pork for 3–4 minutes until browned, in batches if needed. Remove the pork from the pan and set aside on a plate.

Heat the remaining olive oil in the same pan and add the garlic, onion, carrot and celery. Cook, stirring, for 4–5 minutes, until soft and fragrant.

Return the pork to the pan along with the paprika, caraway seeds (if using) and tomato paste. Stir to combine. Add the flour and stir to create a paste. Pour in the beef stock and cook, stirring, for 2 minutes. Bring to a gentle simmer.

Reduce the heat to the lowest setting and cook, covered, for 2½ hours – stirring every 30 minutes – until the pork is fork-tender. Add 125 ml (½ cup) water if the sauce is sticking to the base of the pan.

For the braised red cabbage, heat the olive oil in a large frying pan over medium–high heat. Add the onion and apple and cook, stirring, for 2 minutes until they begin to soften.

Add the red cabbage to the pan and cook for a further 2 minutes until wilted. Add the apple cider vinegar, salt, brown sugar, pepper and 80 ml (⅓ cup) water and cook, stirring, for 1 minute or until the sugar dissolves.

Reduce the heat to the lowest setting, cover and cook for 30 minutes, stirring halfway through cooking. If you find the cabbage is sticking at the halfway mark, add 1–2 tablespoons water. Add the sultanas and cook for a further 15 minutes or until the cabbage is tender.

For the creamy polenta, combine the milk and 500 ml (2 cups) water in a saucepan and bring to the boil. Slowly pour in the polenta and cook, stirring continuously to avoid lumps, for 3–5 minutes until the polenta starts to thicken and come away easily from the side of the pan. Add the butter, parmesan and salt and stir them through.

Serve the polenta immediately with the goulash, braised cabbage, a dollop of sour cream and a sprinkle of parsley (if using).

Honey–garlic slow-cooker chicken

PREP TIME: 10 minutes

COOK TIME: 6 hours

SERVES: 4–6

Leftovers

Refrigerate for up to 2 days. Freeze for up to 2 months. Thaw completely overnight in the fridge before reheating.

I'm pretty picky with what I make in the slow cooker. The ingredients need to be perfectly balanced to create an intense depth of flavour that you would otherwise get from searing and caramelising on the stovetop or in the oven. Anytime I've read a recipe that claims there is 'no need to sear the meat first', I've been sceptical. However, you can trust that in this recipe, although there is no searing in sight, you will be left with the most incredible honey–garlic sauce coating perfectly cooked tender chicken. Being able to 'set and forget' by putting the ingredients in the slow cooker in the morning, then coming home to the aroma of a home-cooked dinner in the afternoon is wonderful. I steam whatever greens I have in the fridge (see page 14 for prep details) and pull out some steamed rice from my freezer (see page 20 for details) to serve along with the chicken.

800 g chicken thigh fillets
2 tablespoons cornflour mixed with 3 tablespoons water
2 spring onions, finely sliced
1 tablespoon sesame seeds
steamed jasmine rice, to serve
steamed greens, to serve

SAUCE
80 ml (⅓ cup) tamari or soy sauce
90 g (⅓ cup) runny honey
2 tablespoons ketchup
2 tablespoons rice wine vinegar
1 tablespoon freshly grated garlic
1 tablespoon freshly grated ginger
1 tablespoon sesame oil

Add the chicken thighs to a slow cooker.

Combine the sauce ingredients in a bowl, then pour the sauce over the chicken. Cook on high for 3–4 hours or on low for 6 hours.

Add the cornflour and water mixture to the sauce for the last 30 minutes of cooking time, basting the chicken with the sauce.

Sprinkle the chicken with the spring onion and sesame seeds and serve with the steamed jasmine rice and steamed greens.

Slow-cooked fall-apart Mexican beef

PREP TIME: 15 minutes

COOK TIME: 3 hours 30 minutes

SERVES: 6–8

We love Mexican food at our place. And when I say Mexican food, I mean all the toppings – and margaritas for Mum and Dad. This is the type of cooking that brings the fun factor of going out into your own home. What I love about this dish is that it can be made ahead, ready to reheat and enjoy. The fall-apart beef in rich, flavour-packed tomato sauce can be served with just about anything – stuffed in burritos or crunchy tacos, piled on corn chips or, my favourite, loaded onto Mexican red rice.

Note

Slow cooker Make the recipe up until the beef is browned and the onion and garlic have been cooked. Add the cooked beef, onion and garlic to the slow cooker along with the remaining ingredients. Cook on low for 10 hours or until the beef is falling apart. Optional: remove the beef from the slow cooker and return the sauce to the stovetop to thicken for 15 minutes over high heat. Shred the beef using two forks and return to the sauce.

Leftovers

Refrigerate the cooked beef for up to 3 days or freeze for up to 3 months. Thaw completely in the fridge overnight before reheating.

Make ahead

This is the perfect recipe to make ahead of time. Refrigerate for up to 3 days or freeze for up to 3 months.

Cook once, eat twice

Repurpose the leftovers and make cheese and rice–filled burritos, tacos or nachos.

1.5 kg chuck steak, gravy beef or oyster blade steak (any slow-cook beef, no need to dice)
2 teaspoons ground cumin
2 teaspoons dried oregano
2 teaspoons sweet paprika
2 teaspoons sea salt flakes
1 teaspoon freshly ground black pepper
1 teaspoon onion powder
1 teaspoon garlic powder
80 ml (⅓ cup) olive oil
1 large onion, finely diced
3 garlic cloves, finely chopped
2 teaspoons tomato paste
400 g can crushed tomatoes

500 ml (2 cups) beef stock
1 teaspoon sugar
juice of 1 lime

SERVING SUGGESTIONS

1 × 250 g Mexican-style microwave rice packet
coriander, tomato and red onion salsa
freshly grated tasty cheese
sour cream
lime wedges
sriracha mayonnaise
diced avocado

Place the beef in a bowl. Add the cumin, oregano, paprika, salt, pepper, onion powder, garlic powder and olive oil and use your hands to evenly coat the meat.

Heat a large, deep frying pan over medium heat and cook the beef in batches for 3–6 minutes until browned. Use 3 tablespoons water to deglaze the pan as needed (if it starts getting sticky). Remove the beef from the pan and set aside.

Add the onion and garlic to the same pan and cook, stirring, for 2–3 minutes.

Add the tomato paste and stir it through, before adding the crushed tomatoes, beef stock, sugar and lime juice. Return the beef to the pan. Bring to the boil, then reduce the heat to the lowest setting. Cook, covered, for 2 hours.

Uncover and cook for a further 1 hour or until the beef can easily be shredded with two forks. If it can't be shredded easily and is still tough, continue cooking in 30-minute intervals. Add 125 ml (½ cup) water if the sauce begins to thicken and catch on the base of the pan.

Remove the beef from the pan, transfer it to a large dish and shred with two forks.

Increase the heat to medium–high and allow the sauce to continue cooking on the stove to thicken, if desired, for 10–15 minutes.

Drizzle the beef with the sauce and serve with your favourite sides.

Fun. Meals to share with a crowd and eat with your hands

Quick & easy san choy bow

PREP TIME: 10 minutes

COOK TIME: 10 minutes

SERVES: 4

Leftovers

Refrigerate the san choy bow filling for up to 3 days. Store the lettuce separately in an airtight container. Not suitable to freeze.

Make ahead

Refrigerate the filling for up to 3 days. Wash, dry and store the lettuce leaves ready for when needed (see page 15 for food storage tips).

Cook once, eat twice

Roll any left-over filling into spring roll pastry wrappers (see page 187) or simply serve on a bed of rice.

This is the ultimate 'catch-all' meal that allows you to use up the vegetables you have in your fridge in the best possible way. Along with pork mince, they are smothered in the most delicious sauce, stuffed into lettuce cups, then sprinkled with crunchy peanuts. San choy bow is fresh and light and one of the easiest meals to prepare – you can have it on the table, with the kitchen wiped down and clear, within 20 minutes. A little bit of chopping is required, but the ease of cooking more than makes up for it. The filling is a great one to prep ahead of time (see page 15) and although I generally nab iceberg lettuce when it's on sale specifically for this meal, you can serve with any lettuce leaves you like. We eat it with sauce dribbling down our arms – it's absolute chaos and so much fun, the kids love it.

1 tablespoon olive oil
1 tablespoon finely chopped garlic
500 g pork mince (or chicken mince)
200 g Swiss brown mushrooms, finely chopped
2 tablespoons tamari or soy sauce
1 teaspoon dark soy sauce
1 tablespoon brown sugar
80 g (½ cup) frozen peas
1 large carrot, peeled and grated
90 g (1 cup) bean sprouts
220 g can water chestnuts, rinsed and drained, finely chopped

125 ml (½ cup) water mixed with 1 tablespoon cornflour
1 spring onion, finely sliced, plus extra to serve
1 tablespoon sesame oil

TO SERVE
iceberg lettuce leaves
crushed peanuts
fried shallots
sliced bird's eye chillies (optional)

Heat the olive oil in a large frying pan over high heat, add the garlic and cook, stirring, for 30 seconds. Add the pork mince and cook, stirring, for 3–4 minutes until browned, breaking it up as you go. Add the mushrooms and cook for a further 2 minutes.

Add the tamari or soy sauce, dark soy sauce and brown sugar to the pan and cook for 2 minutes.

Add the frozen peas, carrot, bean sprouts, water chestnuts, and water and cornflour mixture to the pan and cook, stirring, for 1–2 minutes until the peas have thawed and the sauce has thickened. Add the spring onion and sesame oil and stir them through. Serve heaped in the lettuce cups, topped with the crushed peanuts, fried shallots and chilli (if using).

Pork & fennel sausage rolls

PREP TIME: 10 minutes

COOK TIME: 25 minutes

MAKES: 24

Leftovers

Refrigerate cooked sausage rolls for up to 3 days. Eat warm or cold.

Make ahead

Assemble the sausage rolls as per the recipe but do not brush with egg wash or sprinkle with seasonings. Freeze the uncooked sausage rolls for up to 2 months in an airtight container or reusable sandwich bag, with baking paper between the layers of sausage rolls to stop them sticking. Bake from frozen, adding 15 minutes to the cooking time. Brush with the egg wash and sprinkle with the seasonings before baking.

There is no beating the classic flavour combination of pork and fennel and, combined with crispy pastry, these sausage rolls are really special. Whenever we have a picnic, these are my go-to and used to be highly requested by my family and friends before they all started making them too! They are so incredibly moreish and delicious, and they're so easy that I'm encouraged to make them again and again. They can be made ahead of time and frozen ready for when you need them, so while I've got all the ingredients out I generally make extra and pop them directly into the freezer. It's these simple steps that help give me back time during the week. The kids love these with ketchup (they are even great cold in lunch boxes) whereas I love a good-quality tomato chutney on top. Delish!

2 sheets frozen puff pastry, partially thawed
½ teaspoon sea salt flakes
½ teaspoon white sesame seeds (optional)
½ teaspoon black sesame seeds (optional)
1 teaspoon fennel seeds (optional)
ketchup or tomato chutney, to serve

FILLING
500 g pork mince (substitute with chicken mince, beef mince or lamb mince)
1 teaspoon finely chopped garlic
1 tablespoon Worcestershire sauce
1 tablespoon ketchup
45 g (¾ cup) panko breadcrumbs
1 egg, whisked (reserve 1 tablespoon to brush over pastry)
1 teaspoon sea salt flakes
1 teaspoon fennel seeds

Preheat the oven to 200°C fan-forced.

For the filling, combine all the ingredients (except 1 tablespoon whisked egg) in a large bowl, then use your hands to mix them together well. Divide into four portions.

Cut the thawed puff pastry sheets in half, straight down the middle (you will have four rectangles).

Place a portion of filling in the centre of each piece of puff pastry. Using your hands, shape the filling into a large sausage lengthways along the pastry.

Roll the pastry over the filling into a long log, ensuring the pastry is seam-side down. Cut each log into six equal lengths.

Place the sausage rolls, seam-side down, on a baking tray lined with baking paper – use two trays if required, one on the top rack and one on the bottom.

Brush each sausage roll with the reserved whisked egg. Sprinkle each roll with the salt, sesame seeds and fennel seeds (if using). Bake for 20–25 minutes or until golden. If you have more than one tray in the oven, swap the trays halfway through cooking.

Serve the sausage rolls with the ketchup or tomato chutney.

Beer-battered fish & chips with tartare sauce

PREP TIME: 25 minutes

COOK TIME: 45 minutes

SERVES: 4

Note

Any firm white fish fillets will work with this recipe. My favourites are flathead and whiting but you could use ling, snapper, perch, basa or cod. My recommendation is to let your fishmonger know what you're making, then buy what is in season and on special. If using frozen fillets, allow them to thaw completely in the fridge overnight, then ensure they are as dry as possible using a paper towel.

Leftovers

Fish and chips are best cooked and eaten fresh. Refrigerate left-over tartare sauce for up to 2 days.

Make ahead

You can cut the chips up to 24 hours prior to cooking, then refrigerate completely submerged in cold water. Do not add anything to the water (especially not salt) as the potatoes will go brown. Drain and prepare as per the recipe.

There is nothing that screams 'holidays' or 'the weekend' more than fish and chips and I LOVE being able to bring those vibes home with this homemade version. The takeaway version just can't compete. There is no heavy, thick batter in sight, and once you've made this super-easy tartare sauce it will be hard to go back. The chips are baked in the oven so there's plenty of time to pour yourself a nice cold drink before getting a start on the crispy, golden fish …

TARTARE SAUCE
375 g (1½ cups) whole-egg mayonnaise
1 tablespoon finely diced gherkins
1 tablespoon finely diced capers
1 tablespoon finely diced red onion
1 tablespoon finely chopped dill fronds (or flat-leaf parsley leaves)
1 tablespoon freshly squeezed lemon juice
½ teaspoon sea salt flakes
½ teaspoon freshly ground black pepper

CHIPS
8 sebago potatoes, brushed
3 tablespoons olive oil
1½ teaspoons sea salt flakes

FISH
8 boneless white fish fillets (about 800 g total) (see Note)
35 g (¼ cup) self-raising flour
½ teaspoon sea salt flakes
¼ teaspoon freshly ground black pepper
vegetable oil, for frying
lemon wedges, to serve

BEER BATTER
150 g (1 cup) self-raising flour
40 g (⅓ cup) cornflour
1 teaspoon sea salt flakes
375 ml can fridge-cold beer

For the tartare sauce, combine all the ingredients in a small bowl.

For the chips, preheat the oven to 200°C fan-forced.

Peel the potatoes and cut them into chips roughly 1 cm thick. Submerge the chips in a bowl of cold water as you cut them to stop them going brown. Rinse the chips under cold running water and pat dry well with paper towel.

Arrange the chips on a baking tray – use two trays if needed to avoid overcrowding. Drizzle with the olive oil, sprinkle with the salt and toss well to coat. Bake for 45 minutes, turning once halfway through cooking. If using two trays, place one in the top third and one in the bottom third of the oven and swap halfway through cooking. Once the chips are baked, they need to be eaten immediately (do not leave them sitting in the oven as they will dry out).

Start cooking the fish 10 minutes prior to the chips being ready. Dust the fish with the self-raising flour, salt and pepper.

Combine the beer batter ingredients in a bowl and whisk to mix.

Pour the vegetable oil into a large deep frying pan to a depth of 3 cm and heat over medium–high heat. Slowly lower the fish into the batter, piece by piece, allowing any excess batter to drip off. Place the fish directly in the oil (be careful as it will splatter) – the key is to do it slowly. Cook for 2–3 minutes until golden. Try not to overcrowd the pan as the temperature drop will make the fish less crispy. As the pieces of fish are cooked, place them on a wire rack (set over a tray or sheet of baking paper) to drain. Serve with the chips, tartare sauce and lemon wedges.

Crispy chicken bao buns

PREP TIME: 15 minutes

COOK TIME: 12 minutes

SERVES: 6

Leftovers

Crispy chicken bao buns are best enjoyed immediately, but leftovers can be refrigerated for up to 3 days. Reheat the chicken in a 180°C fan-forced oven for 10–15 minutes to retain its crispiness. Not suitable for freezing.

Make ahead

All vegetables in this dish can be prepared 24 hours prior to serving (see food storage tips on page 15).

Ahh, I really love bao buns! If I ever spotted them on a restaurant menu, I would always order them not realising how easy they are to assemble at home. You can buy fluffy bao buns in the freezer section of the supermarket and pile them high with crispy chicken and a whole heap of fresh veggies. Trust me when I say these are EASY. The veg can be prepared in advance (see page 15 for food storage tips) and the ingredients used in the chicken are simple and impossible to get wrong. It's meals like this that make me feel like I'm never missing out and make me happy to eat in, every night of the week.

2 tablespoons tamari or soy sauce, plus extra to serve
1 teaspoon freshly grated garlic
2 eggs, whisked
500 g chicken thigh fillets, cut into strips across the grain
225 g (1½ cups) plain flour (see Note 1)
1 teaspoon sea salt flakes
½ teaspoon freshly ground black pepper

oil, for frying (see Note 2)
16 bao buns, steamed as per the packet instructions (see Note 3)
2 carrots, julienned or shredded
2 cucumbers, cut into thin batons
½ bunch coriander, leaves picked
125 g (½ cup) sriracha mayonnaise (or regular whole-egg mayonnaise)
2 bird's eye chillies, sliced, to serve (optional)

Place the tamari or soy sauce, garlic, egg and chicken in a bowl, then toss to coat.

Place the flour, salt and pepper in a large bowl. Drain the excess marinade from the chicken, then add the chicken to the flour mixture and toss to coat. Ensure it is fully coated on all sides.

Heat the oil in a large frying pan over medium heat. Cook the chicken in batches for 6–8 minutes, turning once halfway through cooking, then transfer to a plate lined with paper towel to drain.

Serve the bao buns topped with the crispy chicken, carrot, cucumber, coriander, sriracha mayo, a drizzle of tamari or soy sauce, and chilli (if using).

Note 1

This recipe calls for a generous amount of flour as it makes it easier to coat the chicken pieces. You will have some flour left over.

Note 2

Good-quality olive oil can be used for frying, but it does produce a denser, heavier crumb. Vegetable oil and canola oil are best for a light, even crumb. Use a deep, heavy-based frying pan. It needs to be filled at least 3 cm deep with oil.

Note 3

Bao buns can be found in the supermarket freezer section. They are regularly half price so look out for specials! They are traditionally steamed in a basket over boiling water for 7–8 minutes. If you don't have a steamer basket, place three bao buns at a time on a large dinner plate with a mug or small bowl filled with 125 ml (½ cup) water beside them (on the same plate). Cook in the microwave on High in 2-minute intervals until soft and fluffy. Steaming on the stovetop is my preferred method. I use a three-tier steamer basket as I find the buns cook more quickly this way (they are also more fluffy).

Cheesy corn & spring onion fritters

PREP TIME: 5 minutes

COOK TIME: 25 minutes

SERVES: 4 (makes 10)

Note

Fresh corn is the tastiest, but if using frozen corn, thaw it completely before use. Use a scrunched-up paper towel to dry thawed frozen or canned corn prior to use.

Leftovers

Refrigerate for up to 3 days. Freeze for up to 2 months. Thaw completely in the fridge overnight or allow to thaw for 30 minutes on the counter before reheating.

Although there are constantly new trends emerging, I'm a big believer in the classic, simple recipes being the ones that stand the test of time, such as these corn fritters – one of the first ever recipes I shared on social media. They are made with a handful of ingredients (you can use fresh, canned or frozen corn) and you'll find me making a nice big batch of these at least once a fortnight ready for freezing. You can eat them either warm or cold (yay for lunch box options!) and they can be jazzed up with smoked salmon, avocado and a poached egg for a relaxed weekend brunch – although I love them just with sour cream for dipping. The simplicity, flavour and crunch will blow your mind. The recipe calls for 400 g (2 cups) of corn kernels, but you can substitute some of these with another vegetable of choice – grated zucchini, sweet potato, carrot or broccoli are all delicious.

400 g (2 cups) corn kernels, fresh, canned or frozen (see Note)
75 g (½ cup) self-raising flour
½ teaspoon sea salt flakes
1 large egg or 2 small eggs
60 g (½ cup) freshly grated tasty cheese
1 tablespoon full-cream milk, plus extra if needed

2 tablespoons roughly chopped dill fronds
2 spring onions, finely sliced
olive oil, for frying (enough to create a thin layer of oil on the base of the pan)
olive oil spray
sour cream, to serve

Combine the corn, flour, salt, eggs, cheese, milk, dill and spring onion in a bowl. Add a little extra milk if the mixture is too thick.

Heat the olive oil in a large frying pan over medium heat. Spoon ¼ cup corn mixture into the pan and spray the top with olive oil before using your spatula to press the mixture into a flat, circular shape.

Cook two or three fritters at a time – being careful not to overcrowd the pan – for 6–8 minutes, flipping once halfway through cooking. You should get about 10 fritters total. Transfer to a plate lined with paper towel.

Serve the fritters with the sour cream for dipping.

Lemon & oregano chicken tzatziki wrap

PREP TIME: 15 minutes

COOK TIME: 15 minutes

SERVES: 4–6

Note

The water helps to deglaze the pan and create a sticky, caramelised glaze on the chicken. If the chicken is starting to caramelise very quickly and stick to the base of the pan, you can add the water sooner.

Leftovers

Refrigerate left-over chicken for up to 3 days. Not suitable to freeze.

Make ahead

Marinate the chicken up to 24 hours prior to cooking. The tzatziki can be prepared and refrigerated in an airtight container for up to 3 days.

Whenever my husband is craving a kebab, these chicken tzatziki wraps have us covered! Every time I make these I am blown away by how good they taste, especially considering the minimal effort required and simple ingredients used. The marinade on the chicken is sticky and sweet, filled with flavours of garlic, oregano and lemon. The kids can load up with whatever salads they like, which is always a bonus, but I love the combination of tomato and parsley. The homemade tzatziki in this recipe is reason enough to make the chicken, but you could absolutely use store-bought tzatziki to make this an even faster dinner for busy weeknights. The master stroke is meal-prepping the ingredients (cooking the chicken and having the salad ingredients ready, see page 15 for food storage tips) to reheat and stuff directly into wraps on those days that are extra busy.

CHICKEN
500 g chicken thigh fillets
3 tablespoons olive oil
3 tablespoons freshly squeezed lemon juice
1 tablespoon brown sugar
1 teaspoon finely chopped garlic
1 teaspoon sea salt flakes
1 teaspoon sweet paprika
1 teaspoon onion powder
1 teaspoon garlic powder
1 teaspoon dried oregano
½ teaspoon freshly ground black pepper

TZATZIKI
250 g (1 cup) plain Greek yoghurt
1 small cucumber, grated and excess juice squeezed out
1 tablespoon finely chopped dill fronds
1 tablespoon finely chopped mint leaves
1 tablespoon freshly squeezed lemon juice
½ teaspoon freshly grated garlic
½ teaspoon sea salt flakes

TO SERVE
4 medium wraps
¼ bunch flat-leaf parsley, roughly chopped
2 tomatoes, sliced
¼ red onion, sliced

Combine all the chicken ingredients in a large bowl and mix well using your hands or tongs so that the chicken is evenly coated in the marinade.

Combine the tzatziki ingredients in a bowl and set aside.

Heat a large, heavy-based frying pan over medium–high heat and cook the chicken for 10–12 minutes or until cooked through and golden. Turn regularly during cooking and add 125 ml (½ cup) water in the final 2 minutes of cooking (see Note). Slice the chicken into strips, tossing it through the juices in the pan or leave it whole.

Serve the wraps topped with tzatziki, parsley, tomato, the cooked chicken and red onion.

Bang bang prawn tacos

PREP TIME: 15 minutes

COOK TIME: 5 minutes

SERVES: 4

Note

Canola oil, vegetable oil, sunflower oil or similar are best for frying. The oil needs to be at least 2 cm deep so that the prawns are submerged.

Leftovers

Bang bang prawn tacos are best made and eaten immediately.

Make ahead

You can prepare the sauce and salad ingredients in advance (see page 15 for food storage tips) so that all you need to do is cook the prawns (they take minutes!) and warm the tortillas.

Warm Friday nights at our place regularly start with a big batch of these crispy, saucy, fresh little bits of deliciousness. These are seriously good and so quick to prepare; if I've got my vegetables prepped and ready (see page 15 for food storage tips), I can have these on the table within 15 minutes and board games happening soon after. The toppings are of course customisable and if there are sensitive tastes that would prefer no 'bang bang' sauce (which is a decadent mix of mayonnaise, sweet chilli sauce and lime juice), the prawns are equally delicious without it.

24 raw prawns, peeled and deveined
125 ml (½ cup) buttermilk
½ teaspoon sea salt flakes
½ teaspoon sweet paprika
½ teaspoon onion powder
½ teaspoon garlic powder
185 g (1½ cups) cornflour
oil, for frying (see Note)

BANG BANG SAUCE
160 g (⅔ cup) whole-egg mayonnaise
2 tablespoons sweet chilli sauce
2 tablespoons freshly squeezed lime juice

TO SERVE
8 small soft tortillas, warmed
150 g (2 cups) finely shredded red cabbage
½ bunch coriander, leaves picked
200 g grape tomatoes, quartered
lime wedges

Combine the prawns, buttermilk, salt, paprika, onion powder and garlic powder in a large bowl. Toss to coat. Leave to marinate for no longer than 10 minutes.

Place the cornflour in a shallow bowl.

One by one, remove each of the prawns from the marinade, allowing any excess to drip off. Dip them in the cornflour so that all sides are coated, then set aside on a plate. Once coated, the prawns need to be cooked immediately.

Heat the oil in a large frying pan over medium heat. Cook the prawns in batches for 2–3 minutes until golden and cooked through. Transfer to a plate lined with paper towel, using a slotted spoon.

For the bang bang sauce, combine the ingredients in a large bowl. Reserve 125 ml (½ cup) sauce for drizzling on top, then toss the cooked prawns in the remainder of the sauce in the bowl.

Top the warm tortillas with the red cabbage, coriander, tomato and prawns, drizzle on the remaining bang bang sauce and serve with the lime wedges.

Smashed beef burgers with special sauce

PREP TIME: 10 minutes

COOK TIME: 10 minutes

SERVES: 4

Note

The regular beef mince from the supermarket, which is generally 80 per cent lean and 20 per cent fat, is best for super-juicy and flavour-packed patties.

Leftovers

Refrigerate cooked burger patties for up to 3 days. Reheat or eat them cold. They are perfect for lunch boxes.

Make ahead

Freeze raw, uncooked burger patties for up to 2 months (don't add any salt) and thaw completely in the fridge overnight prior to cooking. Prepare your salad ingredients in advance (see food storage tips on page 15).

I add these burgers to my meal plan at least once a fortnight and every time the day rolls around, present me thanks past me for making such an awesome decision. All you need is beef, salt and pepper and around 15 minutes (if that) to make these incredible smashed burgers with crispy edges and juicy, cheese-covered centres. They are made with 100 per cent beef and no fillers – just huge amounts of flavour, especially when served with special burger sauce and a side of wedges (page 190). I love being able to choose the best-quality ingredients that I know are going to taste so much better, and I love the experience of eating burgers at home too. We eat outside, then the kids play in the backyard while we finish our drinks and chat. It is such a beautiful, no-pressure way to enjoy our time together as a family. My toxic trait is adding that burger sauce to everything (I've even added it to pizza, much to the dismay of my husband) but trust me when I say that it's a flavour sensation.

500 g beef mince (see Note)
1 teaspoon sea salt flakes
½ teaspoon freshly ground
    black pepper
1 tablespoon olive oil
4 slices burger cheese
4 burger buns
100 g gherkins, sliced
2 small gem lettuce heads
1 tomato, sliced into rounds
½ red onion, sliced
Crunchy Seasoned Potato Wedges
    (page 190), to serve

SPECIAL BURGER SAUCE
250 g (1 cup) whole-egg mayonnaise
2 tablespoons finely chopped
    gherkins
1 tablespoon ketchup
1 teaspoon dijon mustard
1 teaspoon sweet paprika
1 teaspoon onion powder
1 teaspoon garlic powder
½ teaspoon sea salt flakes

Divide the beef mince into four equal portions and roll each portion into a ball. Once ready to cook, sprinkle with half the salt and pepper – the salt can cause the beef to turn rubbery if left sitting around.

Heat a large frying pan over high heat. Add the olive oil and immediately add one or two of the beef mince balls. Use a spatula to firmly press down on the beef to create thin patties. Cook for 2 minutes, then flip and sprinkle with some of the remaining salt and pepper. Cook for a further 1 minute. Top with a slice of burger cheese. Set aside on a plate. Repeat with the remaining beef mince balls.

Combine the special burger sauce ingredients in a bowl and set aside.

Assemble the burgers in this order: bottom of the bun, burger sauce, gherkins, lettuce, burger patty, cheese, tomato, onion, top of the bun. Serve with the wedges on the side.

Andy's arancini with tomato & basil sauce & smoky aioli

PREP TIME: 35 minutes

COOK TIME: 1 hour

SERVES: 4

Is there anything more delicious than a rice ball with a cheesy, molten centre and a fried, crunchy coating? Andy is my sister-in-law who also happens to be one of my favourite humans on the planet. Over the years we have made (and eaten!) many arancini but these are by far the BEST. Of course there's a little rolling and dredging involved, but the steps in this recipe simplify things (and can even be split across two days) and the whole lot is freezer-friendly. I normally make these in advance with a glass of wine in hand. They always make an appearance when I'm entertaining and trust me when I say that they steal the show every time!

24 cubes tasty cheese
   (approximately 1 cm)
100 g (⅔ cup) plain flour
2 eggs, whisked
240 g (4 cups) panko breadcrumbs
olive oil or canola oil, for frying
   (see Note)
2 tablespoons freshly grated
   parmesan, to serve
basil leaves, to serve

TOMATO AND BASIL SAUCE
2 tablespoons olive oil
1 red onion, finely diced
1 teaspoon finely chopped garlic
2 tablespoons tomato paste
2 x 400 g cans crushed tomatoes
½ bunch basil, leaves picked
2 teaspoons beef stock powder
1 teaspoon white sugar
½ teaspoon sea salt flakes
½ teaspoon freshly ground
   black pepper

SMOKY AIOLI
125 g (½ cup) whole-egg
   mayonnaise
1 tablespoon freshly squeezed
   lemon juice
½ garlic clove, freshly grated
½ teaspoon smoked paprika
½ teaspoon sweet paprika
½ teaspoon sea salt flakes

RISOTTO
2 tablespoons extra-virgin olive oil
1 onion, finely diced
1 teaspoon freshly grated garlic
330 g (1½ cups) arborio rice
125 ml (½ cup) white wine (or
   substitute with additional stock)
1 litre (4 cups) chicken stock
120 g shredded baby spinach leaves
½ teaspoon sea salt flakes
½ teaspoon freshly ground
   black pepper
100 g (1 cup) freshly grated
   parmesan
40 g unsalted butter
2 tablespoons finely chopped
   flat-leaf parsley

Note

The oil needs to be at least 2 cm deep in the base of the pan to shallow-fry the arancini. If you choose to bake the arancini, they will not be the same even, golden brown colour but will definitely be delicious. Heat the oven to 200°C fan-forced, place the arancini on a baking paper–lined tray, spray generously all over with olive oil and bake for 20 minutes.

Hot tip

Make a double batch of the tomato and basil sauce to freeze. It's great stirred through a simple pasta or used with the Spinach & Ricotta Lasagne Parcels (page 84).

Leftovers

Cooked arancini can
be refrigerated for up
to 3 days or frozen for
up to 2 months. Thaw
in the fridge overnight,
then reheat in a 200°C
fan-forced oven for
12–15 minutes until heated
through and crunchy.

Make ahead

Tomato and basil sauce
Can be made ahead, stored
up to 3 days in the fridge
or up to 3 months in the
freezer. Thaw overnight in
the fridge and reheat in
the microwave or on the
stovetop until piping hot.

Smoky aioli Can be
prepared and refrigerated
3 days in advance.

**Assembled uncooked
arancini** Can be
refrigerated for up to
3 days or frozen for up
to 2 months. Thaw in the
fridge overnight and then
cook as per the recipe.

For the tomato and basil sauce, heat the olive oil in a large, deep frying pan over medium–high heat. Add the onion and garlic and cook for 2–3 minutes until softened.

Add the tomato paste and stir it through, then add the crushed tomatoes, basil, beef stock powder, sugar, salt, pepper and 125 ml (½ cup) water. Reduce the heat to the lowest setting and cook, covered, for 30 minutes, stirring occasionally.

For the smoky aioli, combine the ingredients in a bowl and set aside.

Meanwhile, for the risotto, preheat the oven to 180°C fan-forced.

Heat the olive oil a large, oven-proof frying pan over medium heat. Add the onion and garlic and cook for 2 minutes until softened. Add the rice and stir for 1–2 minutes until the grains turn from white to translucent. Add the wine and cook, stirring, for 1–2 minutes until it is mostly evaporated.

Add the chicken stock, spinach, salt and pepper and stir to combine. Bring to a simmer, cover (or transfer to a deep baking tray with a double layer of foil) and bake for 20 minutes. Add the parmesan, butter and parsley and stir them through. It's okay if a little liquid remains as it will absorb as the risotto sits.

Allow the risotto to cool completely before assembling the arancini (overnight in the fridge is best).

To assemble the arancini, roll the risotto into balls (around the size of a golf ball). Push a cheese cube into the centre of each one, using your fingers to seal the arancini around the cheese. Wet your hands if the risotto mixture is sticky. One by one, dredge the arancini in the flour, followed by the whisked egg, then in the panko breadcrumbs, pressing to coat the arancini well.

Heat the oil in a large, deep frying pan over medium–high heat. Cook the arancini in batches for 4–6 minutes until golden and crunchy (see Note for baking instructions).

Dust the arancini with the parmesan, sprinkle on the basil leaves and serve with the tomato and basil dipping sauce and smoky aioli.

Peri-peri chicken burgers

PREP TIME: 10 minutes

COOK TIME: 10 minutes

SERVES: 4

This chicken burger has been a long-standing favourite of mine. It's simple but so delicious, especially when topped with my super-easy peri-peri sauce. The sauce can be made up to 3 days in advance, can be mixed with mayonnaise to make 'perinnaise' and any leftovers also work well as a marinade (coat the chicken pieces and roast for the best peri-peri chicken you'll ever eat in your life!). If you are short on time, and blitzing capsicums just isn't going to happen, you can still absolutely make this. Marinate the chicken in the simple dry rub below, then serve with mayonnaise and the salads of your choice instead – equally delicious!

Note

Capsicum marinated in oil is best but if you can only find roasted capsicum in brine, that's okay too – just use only 1 tablespoon red wine vinegar.

Leftovers

Chicken Refrigerate cooked chicken for up to 3 days. Microwave to reheat. Not suitable to freeze.

Peri-peri sauce Refrigerate for up to 3 days.

Make ahead

Marinate the chicken and refrigerate for up to 3 days before cooking. Freeze for up to 2 months. Thaw completely in the fridge overnight before cooking.

Cook once, eat twice

Reserve 2–3 tablespoons peri-peri sauce to make peri-peri drumsticks. Drizzle 8 drumsticks with the reserved peri-peri sauce, 2 additional tablespoons olive oil and 1 tablespoon sea salt flakes. Bake in a 180°C fan-forced oven, uncovered, for 20 minutes. Add 125 ml (½ cup) water to the pan and turn the chicken before cooking for a further 20 minutes or until cooked through and golden.

2 chicken breast fillets, cut in half horizontally to make 4 steaks
4 burger buns
'Everything' Coleslaw (page 139)
4 slices cheese

MARINADE
1 teaspoon sweet paprika
1 teaspoon sea salt flakes
½ teaspoon dried oregano
½ teaspoon onion powder
½ teaspoon garlic powder
80 ml (⅓ cup) olive oil

PERI-PERI SAUCE
250 g store-bought chargrilled marinated capsicum (see Note)
2 tablespoons red wine vinegar
1 teaspoon sea salt flakes
1½ teaspoons sugar
½ teaspoon finely chopped garlic
½ teaspoon sweet paprika
½ teaspoon dried oregano
½ teaspoon cayenne pepper (optional)
3 tablespoons olive oil

Place the chicken in a bowl along with the marinade ingredients. Use your hands to coat the chicken evenly.

To make the peri-peri sauce, combine all the ingredients, except the olive oil, in a food processor. Blend for 2 minutes, scraping down the side as needed, until smooth. Slowly add the olive oil while blending for a further 1 minute.

Heat a large frying pan over medium heat and cook the chicken for 8–10 minutes. Turn once halfway through cooking and add 2 tablespoons water to help caramelise. Remove the chicken from the pan and set aside to rest on a plate for 2–3 minutes. Serve the chicken in the burger buns with the coleslaw, cheese and peri-peri sauce.

Cheat's birria chicken tacos

Store-bought taco seasoning is more than double the price of this homemade version, which not only takes a couple of minutes to make, but includes wholesome ingredients and tastes 50 times more flavourful than the store-bought stuff! Birria tacos are traditionally made from a slowly cooked, chilli-packed stew. While this version is not traditional (there is no specialty chilli in sight), I've applied some of the same cooking methods that make these tacos so incredibly tasty and worthy of eating any night of the week. The chicken is cooked in a delicious sauce and then shredded before being stuffed into corn tortillas, which are quickly soaked in the cooking sauce before being fried until crisp and golden. The whole lot is topped with a fresh salsa and it's all levels of comforting deliciousness, without any wild prep or huge amounts of time required.

2 tablespoons olive oil
½ red onion, finely chopped
1 teaspoon finely chopped garlic
500 g chicken breast fillet, cut into
   bite-sized pieces
2 teaspoons sweet paprika
2 teaspoons ground cumin
1 teaspoon onion powder
1 teaspoon garlic powder
1 teaspoon dried oregano
1 teaspoon sea salt flakes
½ teaspoon freshly ground
   black pepper
1 tablespoon tomato paste
400 g can crushed tomatoes
olive oil spray
12 mini corn tortillas

125 g (1 cup) freshly grated
   tasty cheese
sour cream, to serve
1 jalapeño, sliced, to serve
   (optional)
lime wedges, to serve

SALSA
2 tomatoes, finely diced
½ red onion, finely diced
½ bunch coriander, finely chopped
1 tablespoon freshly squeezed
   lime juice
½ teaspoon sea salt flakes
¼ teaspoon freshly ground
   black pepper

Heat the olive oil in a large frying pan over medium–high heat. Add the onion and garlic and cook, stirring, for 2 minutes. Add the chicken and cook for 3–4 minutes or until just browned. Add the dried spices and herbs, salt, pepper and tomato paste and stir them through.

Add the crushed tomatoes and 125 ml (½ cup) water and bring to a simmer. Reduce the heat to the lowest setting and simmer for 5–6 minutes, uncovered, or until the chicken is cooked through. Use two forks or the edge of a spatula to shred the chicken into smaller pieces.

Combine the salsa ingredients in a bowl and set aside.

Heat a frying pan over medium–high heat and spray it with olive oil. Working with two tortillas at a time, lightly dip the front and back of each tortilla in the chicken and tomato sauce mixture, then add them to the frying pan. Cook for 1–2 minutes or until golden. Flip and immediately top half of each tortilla with grated cheese and chicken. Fold the top of each tortilla over to form a taco and cook for a further 30 seconds until the cheese is melted. Transfer to a plate. Repeat with the remaining tortillas.

Serve with the salsa, sour cream, sliced jalapeño and the lime wedges.

Zucchini slice with cheese, bacon & corn

PREP TIME: 15 minutes

COOK TIME: 45 minutes

SERVES: 6

Note 1

You can use frozen (no need to thaw), fresh or canned corn for this recipe.

Note 2

Vegetable substitutes This recipe calls for 2½ cups of vegetables, and you can use any you like. Grated carrot, broccoli, cauliflower, sweet potato or finely diced capsicum all work brilliantly.

Leftovers

Zucchini slice can be refrigerated for up to 3 days and frozen for up to 2 months. Thaw completely in the fridge overnight. Reheat in the microwave or eat cold.

For years the kids and I have been having picnics at home. We lay out a small rug in the living room or backyard (weather permitting), our favourite stuffed toys come along and we enjoy all of our favourite picnic foods … one of which is of course zucchini slice. This slice is super-easy to make, can be eaten warm or cold and freezes brilliantly too. It's budget-friendly, takes next to no time to get in the oven and is customisable so you can use vegetables based on what you know your family likes to eat. Whip up this slice on a Sunday to lean into during the week.

½ teaspoon olive oil (to grease the slice tin)
5 eggs, whisked
3 rashers streaky bacon, sliced into small strips
150 g (1 cup) self-raising flour
270 g (2 cups) grated zucchini
100 g (½ cup) corn kernels (optional, see Notes)

125 g (1 cup) freshly grated tasty cheese or any cheddar
40 g (¼ cup) finely diced onion
15 g (¼ cup) finely sliced spring onion
½ teaspoon sea salt flakes
½ teaspoon freshly ground black pepper

Preheat the oven to 180°C fan-forced.

Grease a slice tin (approximately 28 cm x 16 cm) and line it with baking paper.

Combine all the ingredients in a bowl, then spoon the mixture into the tin and level the surface.

Bake the slice for 40–45 minutes or until set and starting to turn golden around the edges. Pierce the centre with a wooden skewer and if it comes out clean, it is cooked.

Allow the slice to stand for 10–15 minutes before slicing and serving.

Crunchy karaage chicken lettuce cups

PREP TIME: 15 minutes

COOK TIME: 10 minutes

SERVES: 4

Note

Good-quality olive oil can be used for frying, but it does produce a denser, heavier crumb.

Vegetable oil and canola oil are best for a light, even crumb. Use a deep, heavy-based frying pan. It needs to be filled at least 3 cm deep with oil.

Leftovers

Refrigerate for up to 3 days. Not suitable to freeze.

Make ahead

Prep the vegetables in advance (check out page 15 for food storage tips).

These crunchy little chicken pieces bundled up in lettuce cups and served with crisp salad, a big squeeze of lemon juice and a dollop of mayo are everything I need and more. Would I make this on a regular night without doing the prep prior? To be completely honest, probably not. I love being able to prepare the salad for dinners like this in advance. That is the beauty of this meal. The lettuce is washed and ready to act as a little vessel for the chicken, the cabbage is shredded and the carrot, spring onion and cucumber are cut so all I'm left to deal with is the chicken, which can be marinated, coated and cooked in 15 minutes flat, leaving me with minimal clean-up and a delicious dinner that the whole family can enjoy.

500 g chicken thigh fillets, thickly sliced
2 tablespoons tamari or soy sauce
1 tablespoon sake
1 teaspoon mirin
1 teaspoon freshly grated ginger
1 teaspoon sugar
½ teaspoon sea salt flakes
¼ teaspoon freshly ground black pepper
125 g (1 cup) cornflour
oil, for frying (see Note)

TO SERVE
2 small gem lettuce heads, leaves separated
1 large carrot, peeled and julienned
75 g (1 cup) shredded green cabbage
1 spring onion, sliced into 6 cm batons
1 cucumber, sliced into 6 cm batons
80 g (⅓ cup) whole-egg mayonnaise
lemon wedges

Place the chicken in a large bowl. Add the tamari or soy sauce, sake, mirin, ginger, sugar, salt and pepper and toss the chicken to coat it well.

Place the cornflour on a baking tray. Piece by piece, dredge the chicken in the cornflour.

Heat the oil in a large frying pan over medium–high heat and cook the chicken in batches for 3–4 minutes, being careful not to overcrowd the pan. Drain the chicken on a plate lined with paper towel.

Top the lettuce leaves with the carrot, cabbage, spring onion, cucumber and chicken. Drizzle with the mayonnaise and serve with the lemon wedges.

Homemade crisp-fried pork spring rolls

PREP TIME: 10 minutes

COOK TIME: 20 minutes

MAKES: 16

Note

Spring roll wrappers can be found in the freezer section of the supermarket. Thaw as per the packet instructions prior to use.

Hot tip

You can form smaller spring rolls by using less filling.

Leftovers

Once cooked, spring rolls are best eaten immediately.

Make ahead

Freeze assembled, uncooked spring rolls for up to 4 weeks. Cook from frozen as per the recipe.

These spring rolls are perfect when I want to use up left-over veggies in my crisper drawer. The veg are cooked in a very simple marinade of garlic and soy sauce, then rolled in store-bought spring roll wrappers. I usually make these rolls as a starter when I'm feeding a crowd – how good are small fried bites and sips of champagne at the beginning of a party? They are inexpensive and I promise they will wow anyone you make them for. You can absolutely serve these with sweet chilli sauce, but for me it's all about plain vinegar. Use a spoon to crack open the centre of the spring roll lengthways, then drizzle some of the vinegar into the filling. It's incredibly delicious.

1 tablespoon olive oil
300 g pork mince (or chicken mince)
250 g bean sprouts
150 g (2 cups) shredded green cabbage
1 large carrot, peeled and shredded
1 teaspoon finely chopped garlic
2 tablespoons tamari or soy sauce
1 teaspoon sugar
½ teaspoon sea salt flakes
½ teaspoon freshly ground black pepper
1 tablespoon sesame oil
16 spring roll wrappers (see Note)
vegetable oil, for frying
3 tablespoons white vinegar or rice wine vinegar with sliced bird's eye chilli and black sesame seeds (optional), to serve

Heat the olive oil in a large, deep frying pan over medium–high heat. Add the pork mince and cook, stirring, for 3–4 minutes until browned, breaking it up as you go. Add the bean sprouts, cabbage, carrot, garlic, 2 tablespoons water, tamari or soy sauce, sugar, salt, pepper and sesame oil. Cook, stirring, for 3–4 minutes until softened. Remove from the heat and allow to cool. Drain off the extra juice.

Assemble the spring rolls by placing a spring roll wrapper in a diamond shape facing towards you. Place ⅓ cup of the filling horizontally across the wrapper. Fold the bottom corner over the filling, then fold in the sides, and then continue rolling from the bottom up. Seal the top by smudging a little water along the seam with your finger.

Heat the vegetable oil in a large frying pan over medium–high heat and fry the spring rolls in batches for 1–2 minutes until golden. Set aside on a plate lined with paper towel to drain.

Serve the spring rolls with the vinegar for dipping (add some sliced chilli and black sesame seeds to this if you like).

Beef quesadillas with avocado cream dip

PREP TIME: 10 minutes

COOK TIME: 20 minutes

SERVES: 4

Note

Instead of making the avocado cream dip, you can serve the quesadillas with sour cream.

Leftovers

Once assembled, beef quesadillas are best cooked and eaten immediately.

Make ahead

Refrigerate for up to 3 days. Freeze the cooked beef mixture for up to 3 months. Thaw completely in the fridge overnight before reheating.

Cook once, eat twice

Enjoy the beef mixture on top of rice or rolled in a burrito.

The delicious mix of beef, capsicum, corn, black beans, spinach and spices in these quesadillas makes this a meal you will want to eat again and again. The beef and black bean mixture is stuffed into a tortilla with cheese, then cooked until crispy in a frying pan. Want to make these completely vegetarian? Double the black beans and omit the beef. If the family isn't keen on capsicum, leave it out. In fact, these quesadillas are completely customisable based on what you have in the fridge. Dip them into sour cream for an easy dinner or, if you're feeling a little adventurous, make the avocado cream dip – a cooling blend of yoghurt, avocado and coriander.

1 tablespoon olive oil
40 g (¼ cup) finely diced onion
1 teaspoon finely chopped garlic
300 g lean beef mince
1 red capsicum, finely diced
100 g (⅔ cup) frozen corn kernels
400 g can black beans, rinsed
   and drained
2 teaspoons sweet paprika
1 teaspoon ground cumin
1 teaspoon onion powder
1 teaspoon dried oregano
1 teaspoon sea salt flakes
½ teaspoon freshly ground
   black pepper
2 tablespoons tomato paste
60 g baby spinach leaves
4 large tortillas
125 g (1 cup) freshly grated
   tasty cheese

AVOCADO CREAM DIP

1 avocado, diced
90 g (⅓ cup) plain yoghurt
½ bunch coriander, roughly chopped
½ teaspoon finely chopped garlic
1 tablespoon freshly squeezed
   lime juice
½ teaspoon sea salt flakes
½ teaspoon freshly ground
   black pepper

Heat the olive oil in a large, heavy-based frying pan over medium–high heat. Add the onion and garlic and cook, stirring, for 2–3 minutes.

Add the beef mince to the pan and cook for 3–4 minutes until browned, breaking it up as you go. Add the capsicum, corn, black beans, paprika, cumin, onion powder, oregano, salt, pepper and tomato paste and stir them through. Add the spinach leaves and, once they are wilted, add 3 tablespoons water. Reduce the heat to the lowest setting and simmer over low heat for 5–6 minutes.

To make the avocado cream dip, combine the ingredients in a food processor. Blend until smooth, adding 1–2 tablespoons water to thin if required.

To assemble the quesadillas, heat the tortillas one by one in a large frying pan over medium heat for 30 seconds, flipping it over halfway through. Spoon one-quarter of the filling onto one half of the tortilla and top with one-quarter of the cheese. Fold the empty side of the tortilla over to enclose the filling. Use your spatula to quickly flip the tortilla over. Cook for 1 minute or until crispy. Remove from the pan, allow to cool slightly and cut into three. Serve with the avocado cream dip (see Note) for dipping.

Crunchy seasoned potato wedges

PREP TIME: 8 minutes

COOK TIME: 45 minutes

SERVES: 4

Note

This recipe works with any potato variety – including waxy potatoes. The results are always crispy on the outside and soft and fluffy on the inside. The recipe doesn't call for the potatoes to be peeled (it's one less step, and the skin is packed with nutrients), but you can peel them if you wish. Cut your potatoes into wedges by halving lengthways, cutting each half in half again and then, for large potatoes, cutting each wedge in half again to give you a total of eight pieces.

Leftovers

Best cooked and served immediately. Leftovers can be refrigerated for up to 3 days and reheated in the microwave or oven.

Make ahead

Cut potatoes up to 24 hours before cooking. Store refrigerated, fully submerged in water (do not add salt or flavouring to the potatoes as this will cause them to brown). Once ready to cook, drain and pat dry with paper towel.

Is it possible to make homemade delicious, seasoned wedges in the oven that are crunchy and crispy every single time? It is! We serve these with everything – from homemade burgers and schnitzels, to fish and grilled chicken, steak or skewers on the barbecue. They are so versatile and easy to make. No deep-frying, no fancy potato varieties, no unrecognisable ingredients and no fuss. You don't need to peel the potatoes if you don't want to (I slowly started leaving a few potatoes unpeeled in each batch of wedges and gradually my family stopped noticing) and you'll be left with perfect wedges ready to be dipped in sour cream and sweet chilli. The best!

1.2 kg unpeeled potatoes, cut into wedges (see Note)
2 teaspoons sea salt flakes
1 teaspoon sweet paprika
1 teaspoon garlic powder
1 teaspoon onion powder
½ teaspoon freshly ground black pepper
3 tablespoons olive oil, plus extra if needed
sweet chilli sauce, to serve
sour cream, to serve

Preheat the oven to 200°C fan-forced.

Arrange the cut potatoes on a baking tray large enough so the wedges are not overlapping. Use two trays if you need to, placing one on the top rack and one on the bottom rack of the oven, but you'll need to swap the trays halfway through cooking.

Sprinkle the wedges with the salt, paprika, garlic powder, onion powder and pepper. Use your hands to coat them evenly with the spice mix – this is the key to the spices not clumping together.

Drizzle the wedges with the olive oil, then use your hands to coat further so that the spices are as evenly distributed as possible. If they are still clumping, use a little more olive oil. Arrange the wedges on the baking tray, cut-side down. Bake for 45 minutes or until the wedges are golden, turning once halfway through cooking.

Serve the wedges with the sweet chilli sauce and sour cream.

Prawn rice paper rolls with hoisin–peanut sauce

PREP TIME: 30 minutes

COOK TIME: nil

SERVES: 4 (makes 12)

Leftovers

Place left-over rolls in an airtight container, taking care to not overlap them. Cover them with a damp paper towel before replacing the lid. Store for up to 24 hours.

Make ahead

Assembled rice paper rolls can be refrigerated for up to 24 hours in advance. Store as above.

I absolutely love rice paper rolls. The freshness of the vegetables combined with the hoisin–peanut dipping sauce is so moreish and delicious. Rice paper is inexpensive, easy to find and not at all hard to work with. I make these all the time, particularly when I'm entertaining. Although my rolls always come out a little wonky, in different shapes and sizes, no one cares and they are the first thing to be eaten every single time! These are equally delicious with left-over roast chicken (page 54) or tofu. If you haven't tried making these before, this is your sign to give them a go.

12 sheets round rice paper
18 cooked prawns, cleaned and
   deveined, cut in half lengthways
½ bunch coriander, leaves picked
½ bunch mint, leaves picked
100 g rice vermicelli noodles
   (cooked as per the packet
   instructions)
75 g (1 cup) shredded red cabbage
1 carrot, peeled and julienned
lime wedges and finely sliced spring
   onion, to serve

HOISIN–PEANUT SAUCE
3 tablespoons hoisin sauce
2 tablespoons natural smooth
   peanut butter
1 tablespoon rice wine vinegar or
   freshly squeezed lime juice
1 teaspoon sesame oil
2 tablespoons water
1 tablespoon crushed peanuts,
   to serve

Soak the rice paper sheets, one at a time, as per the packet instructions. As a general guide, soak in warm water for 5 seconds, then place on a damp tea towel to soften for 30 seconds. The rice paper sheet is then ready to use.

Arrange the fillings, starting with whatever you want to see on the top of the rice paper roll. I first add the prawns, then the herbs, then the remaining ingredients.

Place the fillings on the bottom third of the rice paper. Fold the bottom edge of the rice paper over the filling, fold in the sides, then roll up to enclose. Place on a serving plate, seam-side down.

For the hoisin–peanut sauce, use a whisk to combine the ingredients in a bowl. Add more water if required, to achieve your desired consistency (this will depend on the thickness of the peanut butter used). As more water is added, the sauce will become paler and thinner.

Sprinkle the sauce with the crushed peanuts, sprinkle the rice paper rolls with spring onion and serve with lime wedges on the side.

Fish tacos with corn & avocado salsa

PREP TIME: 20 minutes

COOK TIME: 8 minutes

SERVES: 4

Note 1

Any firm white fish fillets will work here. I like flathead and whiting but you could use ling, snapper, perch, basa or cod, though larger fillets will need to be cut to size. If using frozen fillets, allow them to thaw completely in the fridge overnight, then dry with paper towel.

Note 2

Char your corn using a gas burner. Remove the husk and, using tongs, hold the steamed corn over the flames on medium–high heat. Turn every few seconds until the corn is charred on all sides. Alternatively, heat a chargrill pan over high heat and cook the corn for 2–3 minutes, turning regularly until charred.

Leftovers

Best eaten immediately.

Make ahead

Prepare the cabbage ahead of time (see the food storage tips on page 15).

Cook once, eat twice

Serve the grilled fish with the chips and tartare sauce on page 163.

One of my favourite meals to eat out used to be fish tacos until I started making them at home – realising that not only were they much tastier, fresher and lighter, but also a fraction of the price … and it gave me the ability to drizzle unlimited sriracha mayo over them. My family absolutely loves these and, being pan-fried in a little olive oil and flour, they still have the crispy factor without the heaviness of being deep-fried. Fish is a protein that takes minutes to cook and paired with some pre-prepared salads (see page 15), you have got an incredibly delicious and fast dinner suited to any night of the week.

8 small firm white fish fillets (about 600 g total) (see Note 1)
1 teaspoon sweet paprika
1 teaspoon sea salt flakes
½ teaspoon freshly ground black pepper
75 g (½ cup) plain flour
olive oil, for frying (enough to form a thin layer on the base of the pan)

CORN AND AVOCADO SALSA
1 fresh corn cob, husk intact
1 bunch coriander, roughly chopped
1 avocado, cut into small cubes
1 tablespoon freshly squeezed lime juice
1 teaspoon sea salt flakes

TO SERVE
8 small flour tortillas
sriracha mayonnaise
75 g (1 cup) shredded red cabbage
sliced jalapeño, to serve
lime wedges, to serve

Place the fish flat on a plate and pat dry with scrunched-up paper towel. Sprinkle with half the paprika, salt and pepper. Flip and repeat on the other side with the remaining paprika, salt and pepper.

Place the flour on a baking tray. Press the fish into the flour on both sides and shake off any excess.

Heat the olive oil in a large frying pan over medium–high heat and cook the fish in batches for 6–8 minutes, turning once halfway through cooking. Set aside on a plate lined with paper towel to drain.

For the corn and avocado salsa, heat the corn in its husk in the microwave on High for 2–3 minutes (place the corn directly on the microwave turntable). Alternatively, the corn can be steamed or placed in boiling water for 2–3 minutes (see Note 2 for charred corn). Remove the husks and cut the kernels off the cob using a sharp knife, then toss the kernels with the remaining ingredients. Set aside.

Serve the flour tortillas topped with the sriracha mayonnaise, red cabbage, the cooked fish, the corn and avocado salsa and the sliced jalapeño with a side of lime wedges.

Conversion charts

Measuring cups and spoons may vary slightly from one country to another, but the difference is generally not enough to affect a recipe. All cup and spoon measures are level.

One Australian metric measuring cup holds 250 ml (8 fl oz), one Australian metric tablespoon holds 20 ml (4 teaspoons) and one Australian metric teaspoon holds 5 ml. North America, New Zealand and the UK use a 15 ml (3-teaspoon) tablespoon.

LENGTH

METRIC	IMPERIAL
3 mm	⅛ inch
6 mm	¼ inch
1 cm	½ inch
2.5 cm	1 inch
5 cm	2 inches
18 cm	7 inches
20 cm	8 inches
23 cm	9 inches
25 cm	10 inches
30 cm	12 inches

LIQUID MEASURES

ONE AMERICAN PINT	ONE IMPERIAL PINT
500 ml (16 fl oz)	600 ml (20 fl oz)

CUP	METRIC	IMPERIAL
⅛ cup	30 ml	1 fl oz
¼ cup	60 ml	2 fl oz
⅓ cup	80 ml	2½ fl oz
½ cup	125 ml	4 fl oz
⅔ cup	160 ml	5 fl oz
¾ cup	180 ml	6 fl oz
1 cup	250 ml	8 fl oz
2 cups	500 ml	16 fl oz
2¼ cups	560 ml	20 fl oz
4 cups	1 litre	32 fl oz

DRY MEASURES

The most accurate way to measure dry ingredients is to weigh them. However, if using a cup, add the ingredient loosely to the cup and level with a knife; don't compact the ingredient unless the recipe requests 'firmly packed'.

METRIC	IMPERIAL
15 g	½ oz
30 g	1 oz
60 g	2 oz
125 g	4 oz (¼ lb)
185 g	6 oz
250 g	8 oz (½ lb)
375 g	12 oz (¾ lb)
500 g	16 oz (1 lb)
1 kg	32 oz (2 lb)

OVEN TEMPERATURES

CELSIUS	FAHRENHEIT
100°C	200°F
120°C	250°F
150°C	300°F
160°C	325°F
180°C	350°F
200°C	400°F
220°C	425°F

CELSIUS	GAS MARK
110°C	¼
130°C	½
140°C	1
150°C	2
170°C	3
180°C	4
190°C	5
200°C	6
220°C	7
230°C	8
240°C	9
250°C	10

A big thank you!

Sharing the meals I prepare for my family through my social media channels over the last few years has brought me so much joy, but I never dreamed I would have the opportunity to share these recipes in a book. Not realising how many moving parts there are to publishing, I've found myself captivated by the experience. It's been soul-enriching seeing this incredible project come to life. So much love has gone into planning, writing, cooking, designing and shooting this book, and it would not have been possible without these very special people.

To my husband, without you, none of this would exist. I know I tease you for getting a haircut, mowing the lawn or spending hours in the garage right before guests are coming over, but I secretly love it and wouldn't have it any other way. You put up with my need to declutter everything we own and my irrational fear of wasps … and bees … and spiders. But who's counting? I am grateful for every minute I get to spend with you, especially the minutes while you're barbecuing and I'm doing nothing. Thank you for being my biggest supporter and for always making me laugh. Life is amazing because of you, and I've been able to do this because of you.

To my little boy and little girl, you are my reasons why. You are my favourite people on the planet and I feel so lucky to be able to spend my days with you. Sitting down to dinner and watching you dip dumplings into soy sauce and twirl spaghetti around your forks with gusto is the best way to end a day. I'm so incredibly proud watching you grow into the loving, kind, funny and generous souls that you are. I love you more than anything and everything I do is because of you.

Mum and Dad, I love the joy you get from swimming in the ocean and being outdoors fishing. I love how resourceful you are, spending time fixing even those items that are easily replaceable. And I love that you prioritise sourcing the best-value, best-quality ingredients so that you can make the incredible, nostalgic recipes that we love so much. You have taught me everything I know, including how to value the simple things in life. I'll forever be grateful … and I'll always be your little girl.

To my brother, Roman, you have always been, and will always be, the calm in the storm. Your wisdom, guidance and ability to soothe my ailments within minutes is a life skill. Growing up, I thought you were so clever and cool, and you'll be happy to know that not only do I still think you're one of the cleverest people I know … but I still think you're super cool. Our time spent together means more to me than you will ever know. And to your beautiful wife and my nephew and niece, I am so proud of you and thank you for your never-ending support and encouragement.

Andy, I hit the jackpot marrying your brother because I inherited you. You are my best friend, my voice of reason and my biggest cheerleader. You have always believed in me more than I believed in myself. I will forever yell at you and restrain you with what you call my 'superhuman strength' while you scold me for my impossibly poor fashion choices. Thank you for rallying behind me and giving me the push that I needed to make this happen. I am so grateful for you.

Nanny, Uncle Mike, Grandpa Lolo and Lola. Your families have taught me so much about food. From Nanna's curry puffs to Granny's traditional pork roast, these are such incredible memories that I will hold onto for life. I feel so incredibly blessed and grateful to be a part of your family … and you're also the best unofficial taste-testers!

Biggest love to you, Nicola, for tirelessly cooking up a storm with me in my kitchen (I'm sure you grated 100 onions!). I loved our chats and I will forever be grateful for your generosity and willingness to help me bring my dream to life.

To Mary Small, my amazing publisher, we quite literally would not be here if it wasn't for you. Within minutes of chatting to you, I felt like I'd known you my whole life. I adore you and absolutely love working with you. I knew this book would take me far out of my comfort zone, yet during the entire process, your belief and calm energy gave me the confidence I needed to not only get through it, but also enjoy it. I am so grateful for you and thank you so much for your trust in me.

Thank you to Clare Marshall, my incredible project editor, for all your hard work on the book. You have been such a dream to work with and have made the process so seamless.

Huge thanks to my editor, Ariana Klepac. Your expertise, eye for detail, thoroughness and encouragement along the way have made this book what it is and I could not have done it without you.

Madeleine Kane, thank you for the genius design that has brought the book to life and for very much capturing 'me'.

To Jeremy Simons, your ability to see beauty in the ordinary is such an incredible gift. There are the people who walk past an old wooden trolley and then there are those who see its divinity and move the earth to take it home with them. I feel honoured to have had the opportunity to work with you. Nothing was ever too difficult, and your patience and generosity are so incredibly admirable. Thank you for your beautiful photography, you are a legend!

To Deb Kaloper, my incredibly talented, beautiful stylist. I feel so lucky to have spent time watching you do what you do. I observed in awe as you delicately pieced together my recipes with patience, precision and an air of effortlessness. I learned so much from you and feel grateful to have spent time in your calming and comforting presence. I find myself operating more mindfully and channelling you whenever I feel rushed or stressed. What you have created is spectacular and I can't thank you enough. You are the absolute best!

To Kerrie Ray, Jimmy Callaway and Claire Dickson-Smith. Wow, wow, wow. Thank you so much for working so tirelessly in the kitchen. Your organisation and your ability to charge through those long days the way you did was so incredibly inspiring and I am so grateful. You made such a fantastic team and so much work went into it all. Thank you. You are a beautiful bunch of people.

Thank you to Ecology Homewares for providing me with many of your amazing products over the years and for helping me bring my recipes to life.

And lastly, the biggest thanks to those of you who have been with me on my journey at Simple Home Edit from the very beginning. Aside from helping me with all of life's decisions (where would I be without your guidance around my footwear choices?), you truly provide me with the encouragement and energy to keep going. You give me purpose and you are such a big part of my life. Thank you so much for your continued support (which bewilders me on the daily) and for all the laughs. I am grateful for each and every one of you and your friendship.

Nic x

Index

Pan Macmillan acknowledges the Traditional Custodians of Country throughout Australia and their connections to lands, waters and communities. We pay our respect to Elders past and present and extend that respect to all Aboriginal and Torres Strait Islander peoples today. We honour more than sixty thousand years of storytelling, art and culture.

A Plum book
First published in 2024 by
Pan Macmillan Australia Pty Limited
Level 25, 1 Market Street,
Sydney, NSW 2000, Australia

Level 3, 112 Wellington Parade,
East Melbourne, VIC 3002, Australia

Designed and typeset by Madeleine Kane
Edited by Ariana Klepac
Index by Max McMaster
Photography by Jeremy Simons, with additional photography by Nicole Maguire
Food and prop styling by Deborah Kaloper
Food preparation by James Callaway, Claire Dickson-Smith and Kerrie Ray

Colour reproduction by Splitting Image Colour Studio
Printed and bound in China by 1010 Printing International Limited

A CIP catalogue record for this book is available from the National Library of Australia.

The publisher would like to thank the following for their generosity in providing props for the book: Slip Ceramics.

10 9 8 7 6 5